C000214764

RBY·DERBY

ESTATE PUBLICATIONS
Bridewell House,
Tenterden,Kent.
TN30 6EP
Tel:01580 764225

Loscoe
22   23
HEANOR

A610

A6007

A6

A38

Duffield
26

Little
Eaton
7

A608

A6096

Allestree
Breadsall
Oakwood
8   9   10   11
Markeaton
Chaddesden

A52

Ockbrook

6
DERBY
Spondon
16   17
12   13
14   15
Mickleover
Borrowash

A52

M1

27
Draycott

Normanton
Alvaston
18   19   20   21
Osmaston
A6
Sinfin
Allenton
Findern
27
Chellaston

A50

A50

Lockington
CASTLE
DONINGTON
24   25
23

ROAD MAP   page 4-5
ENLARGED CENTRE   page 6
STREET INDEX   page 28

A453

E S T A T E   P U B L I C A T I O N S

DERBY

HEANOR · DUFFIELD · CASTLE DONINGTON
MICKLEOVER · CHELLASTON · BORROWASH

Every effort has been made to verify the accuracy of information in this book but the publishers cannot accept responsibility for expense or loss caused by any error or omission. Information that will be of assistance to the user of the maps will be welcomed.

The representation of a road, track or footpath on the maps in this atlas is no evidence of the existence of a right of way.

One-way Street	←
Car Park	P
Place of Worship	✦
Post Office	●
Public Convenience	C
Pedestrianized	▨

Scale of street plans 3½ inches to 1 mile
Unless otherwise stated

Street plans prepared and published by ESTATE PUBLICATIONS, Bridewell House, TENTERDEN, KENT, and based upon the ORDNANCE SURVEY mapping with the permission of The Controller of H. M. Stationery Office.

The publishers acknowledge the co-operation of the local authorities of towns represented in this atlas.

Estate Publications 179 H   ISBN 1 84192 004 5   © Crown Copyright 398713

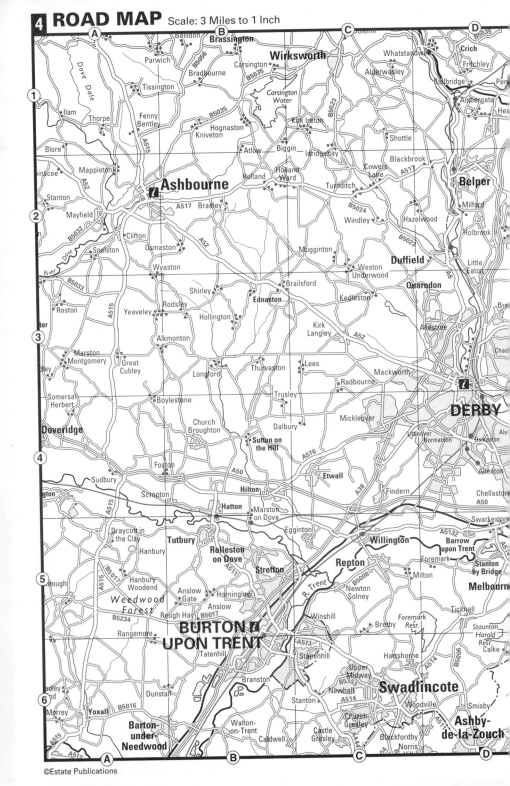

4 ROAD MAP Scale: 3 Miles to 1 Inch

©Estate Publications

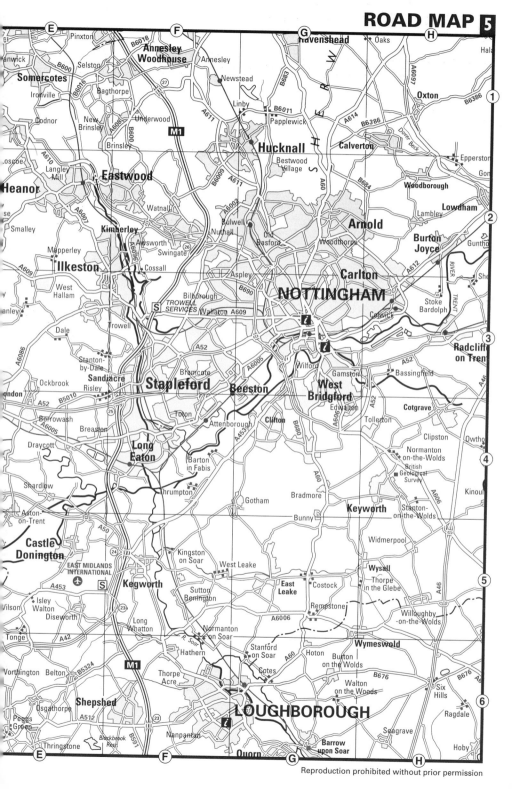

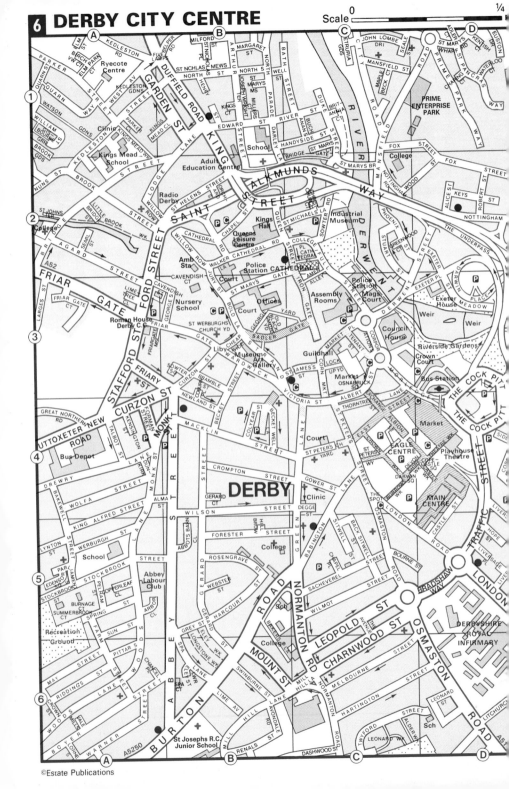

Scale 0 ——— ¼

DERBY

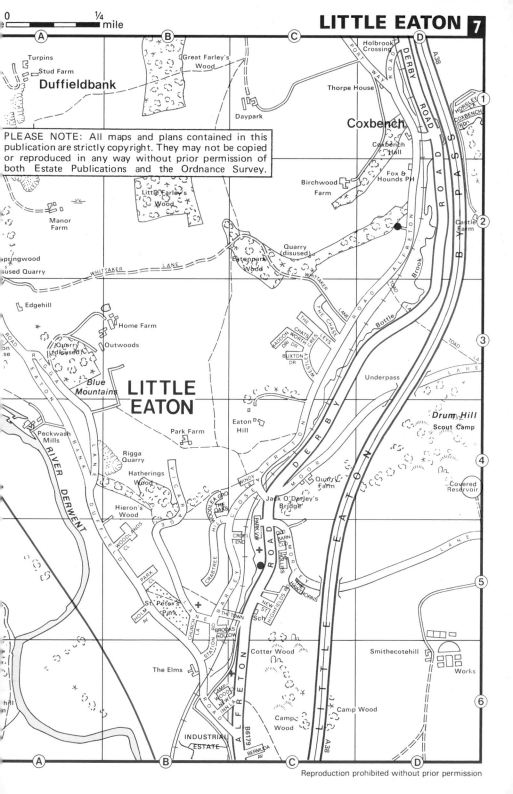

0 ¼ mile

A   B   C   D

Turpins
Stud Farm
Duffieldbank

Great Farley's
Wood

Holbrook
Crossing

Thorpe House

1

Daypark

Coxbench

HORSLEY PK
COXBENCH RD

Coxbench
Hall

Little Farley's
Wood

Birchwood
Farm

Fox &
Hounds PH

Manor
Farm

Quarry
(disused)

Castle
Farm

2

Springwood
Disused Quarry

Eatenpark
Wood

WHITTAKER   LANE

WHITTAKER   LANE

Bottle Brook

Edgehill

Home Farm

Outwoods

Quarry
(disused)

THE CHASE

CHATSWORTH DR

HADDON DR

BUXTON DR

WHISTLESTONE

LANE

Underpass

TOAD LANE

3

**Blue
Mountains**

LITTLE
EATON

Peckwash
Mills

Park Farm

Rigga
Quarry

Hatherings
Wood

Eaton
Hill

Drum Hill
Scout Camp

4

Covered
Reservoir

RIVER DERWENT

RIGGA LANE

EATON BANK

DUFFIELD ROAD

VICARAGE RD

Hieron's
Wood

WOODLANDS CL

Quarry
Farm

WINDY LA

THE OAKS

WOODLEA GRO

HILL CLOSE

Jack O'Darley's
Bridge

MORLEY LANE

MOOR ROAD

DERBY ROAD

ALFRETON ROAD

PARK CL

BARLEY LANE

CRABTREE

CROFT END

PARK VW

BARN CL

THE HOLLIES

LANE

5

St Peter's
Park

HOLME AV

CHURCH LA

STATION ROAD

THE TOWN

BROOKS HOLLOW

NEW ST

HIGHFIELDS RD

Sch

HAWTHORNS

Smithecotehill

Works

The Elms

Cotter Wood

CAMP WOOD VIEW

NEW INN LA

BERMUDA AV

B6179

ALFRETON ROAD

Campc
Wood

Camp Wood

6

INDUSTRIAL
ESTATE

A   B   C   D

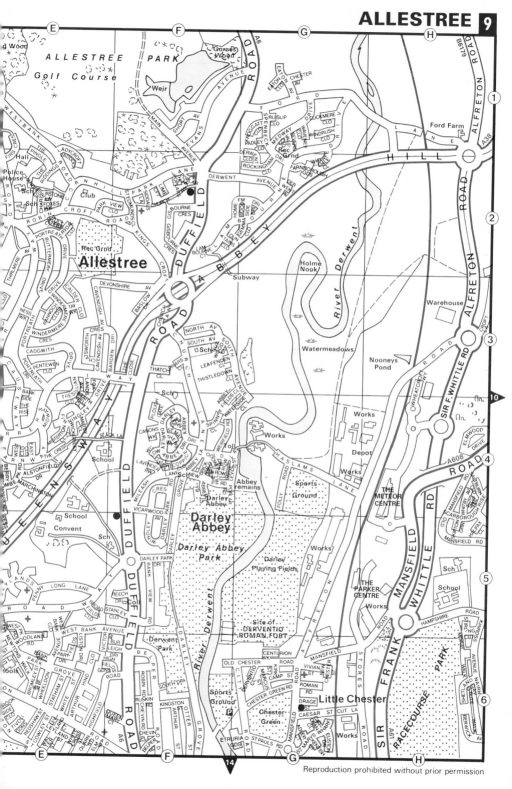

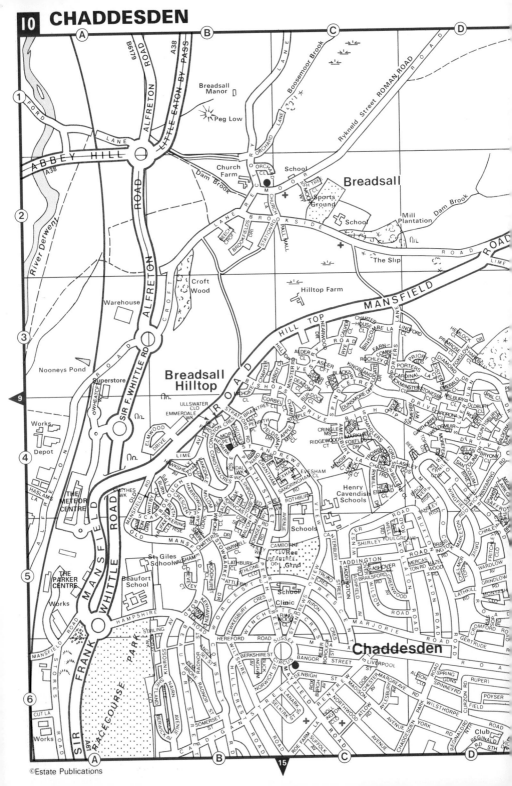

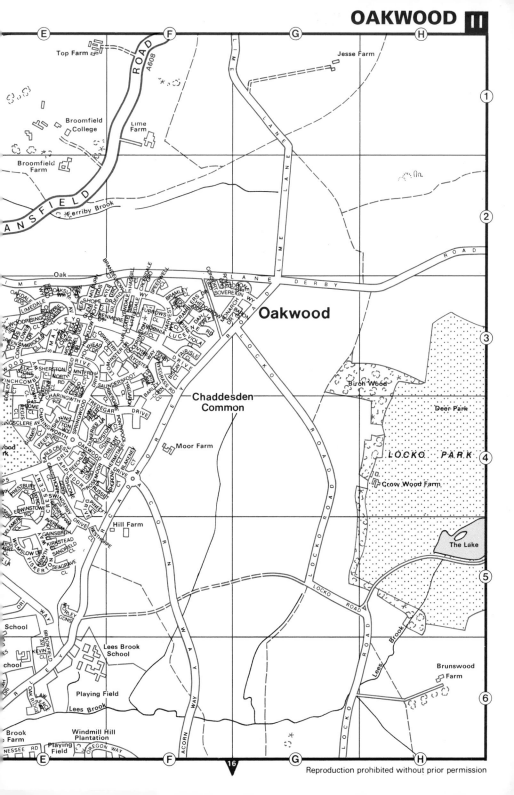

OAKWOOD

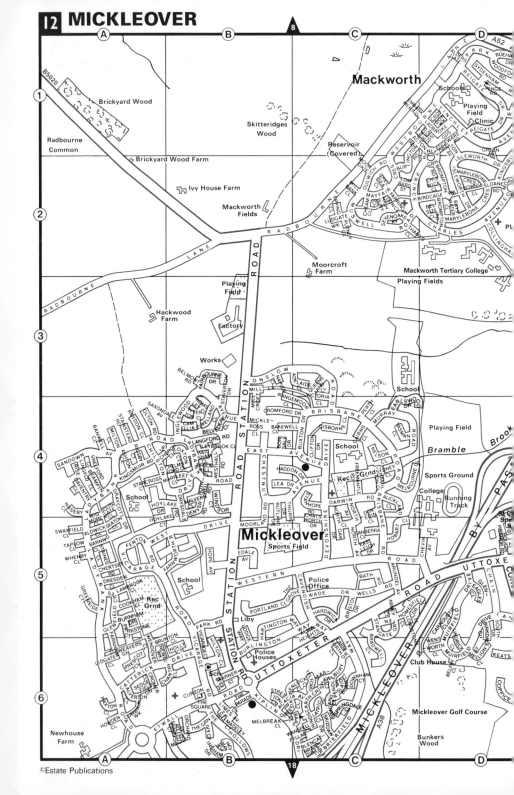

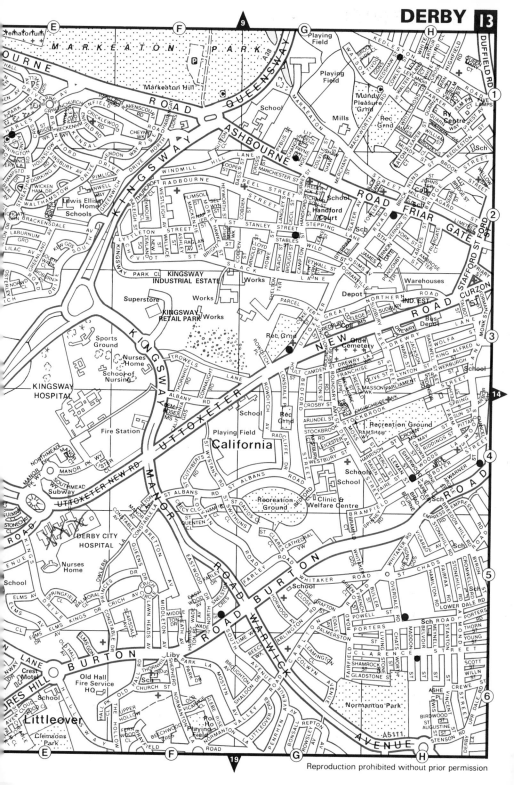

DERBY 13

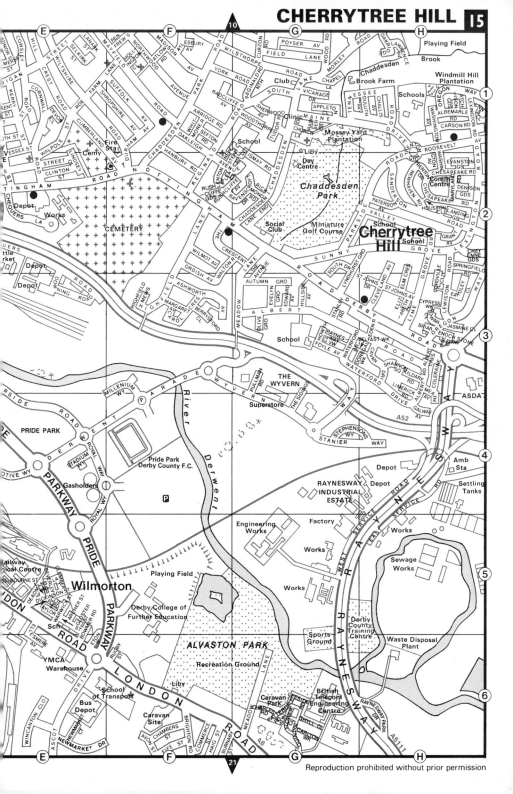

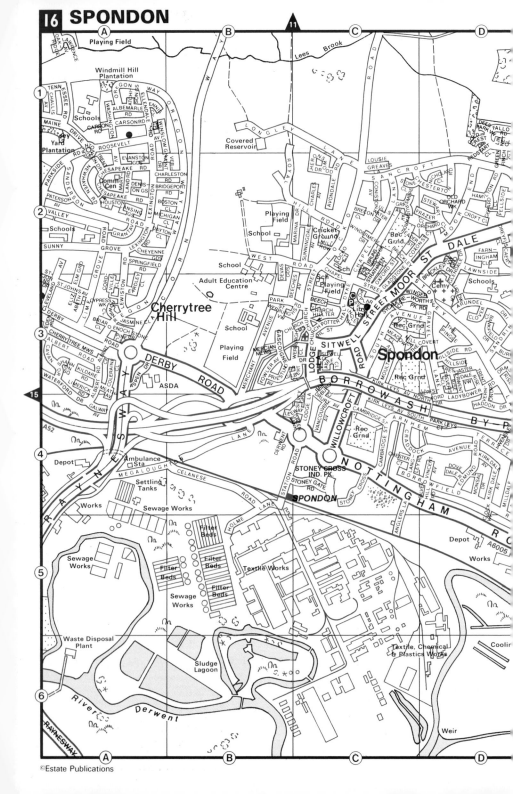

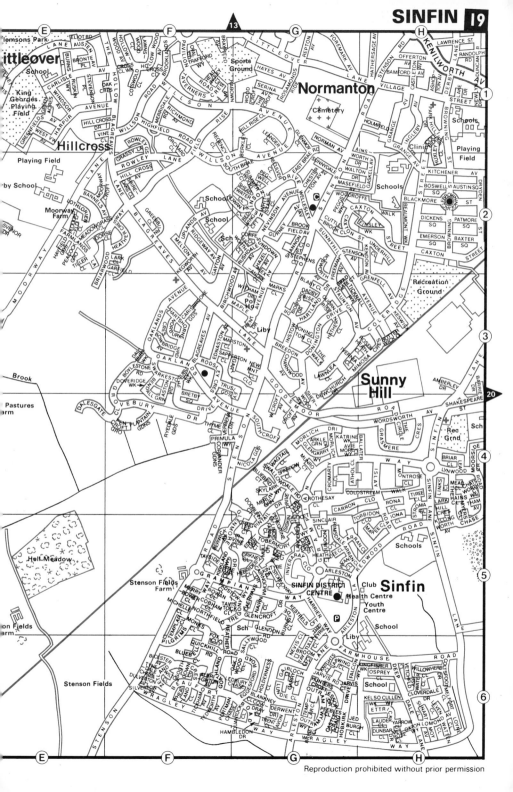

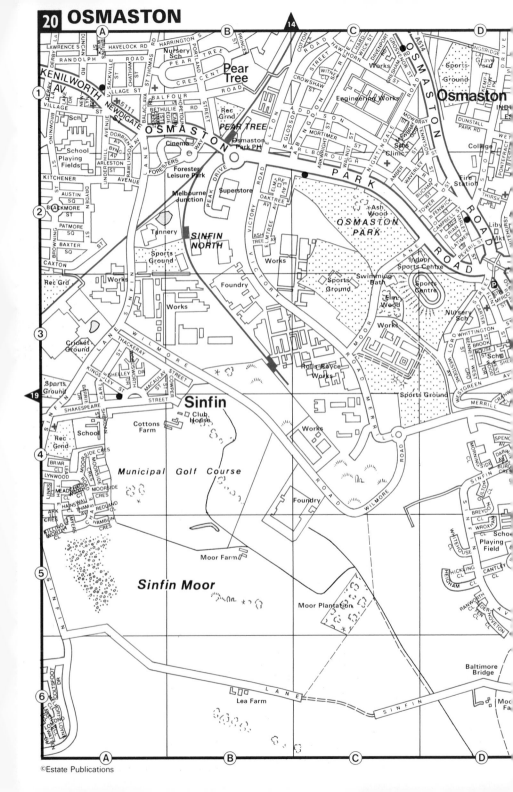

©Estate Publications

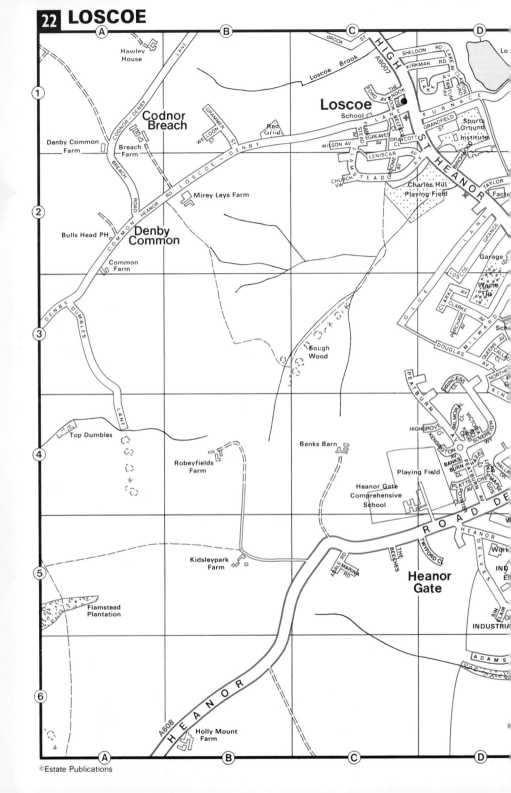

Hawley House

Codnor Breach

Denby Common Farm

Breach Farm

Bulls Head PH

Denby Common

Common Farm

Denby Dumbles

Top Dumbles

Robeyfields Farm

Kidsleypark Farm

Flamstead Plantation

Mirey Leys Farm

Sough Wood

Banks Barn

Holly Mount Farm

Loscoe Brook

BROOK ST

HIGH ST

A6007

SHELDON RD

KIRKMAN RD

Loscoe

School

Red Grill

WILSON AV

LENISCAR

Charles Hill Playing Field

Sports Ground

Institute

TAYLOR

Garage

Waste Tip

Sough Wood

HIGHGROVE

Playing Field

Heanor Gate Comprehensive School

THE BEECHES

Heanor Gate

Work

IND E

INDUSTRI

ADAMS

HEANOR RD

A608 HEANOR

ST HEANOR

ROAD DE

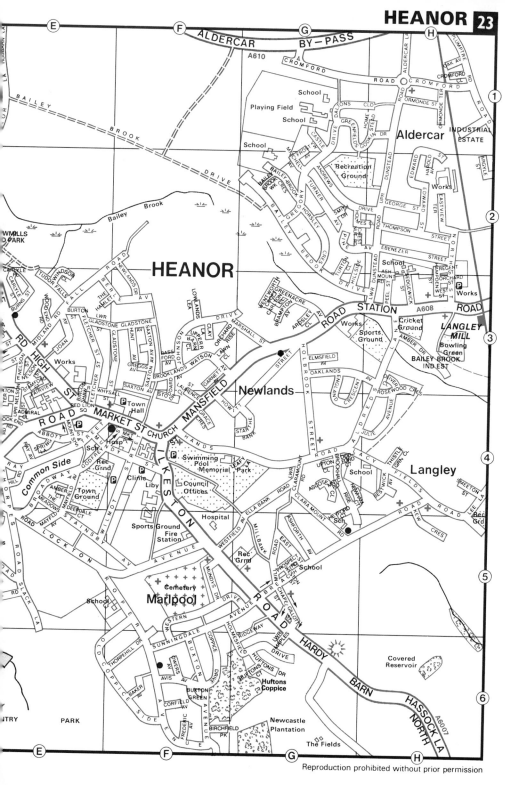

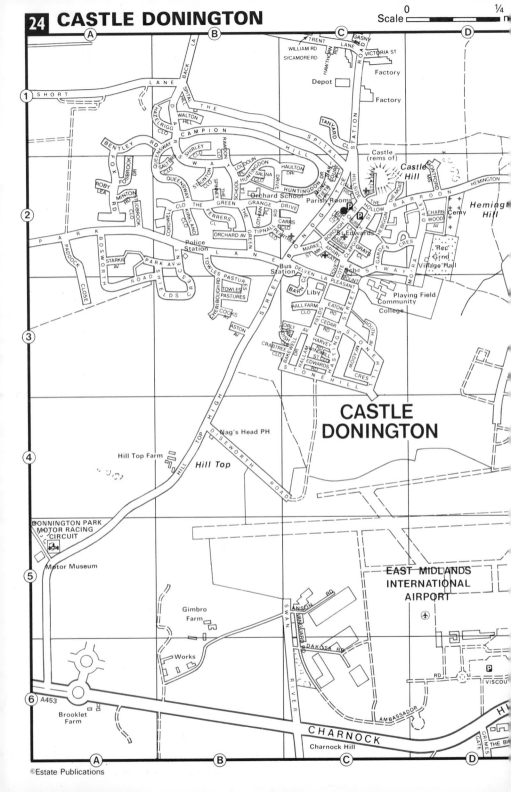

Scale 0 — ¼ mi

CASTLE DONINGTON

EAST MIDLANDS
INTERNATIONAL
AIRPORT

DONINGTON PARK
MOTOR RACING
CIRCUIT

Motor Museum

Hill Top

Hill Top Farm

Nag's Head PH

Gimbro Farm

Works

Brooklet Farm

A453

CHARNOCK

Charnock Hill

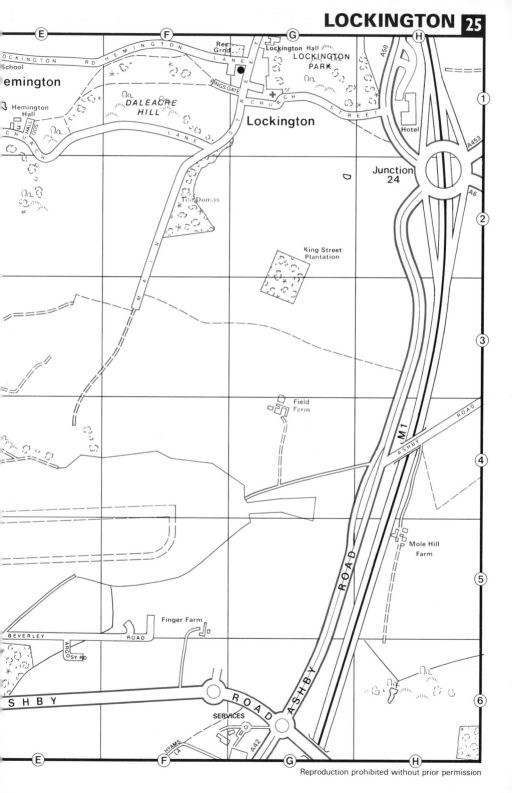

E   F   G   H

OCKINGTON   RD   HEMINGTON   LANE   Rec
School   Grid

Lockington Hall
LOCKINGTON
PARK

emington   KINGS GATE

DALEACRE
HILL   CHURCH

Hemington   Lockington
Hall

LANE

The Dumps

Junction
24

Hotel

A50
A453
A6

1

2

King Street
Plantation

3

Field
Farm

ROAD

M1

ASHBY

4

Mole Hill
Farm

5

ROAD

BEVERLEY

ARGOSY RD

Finger Farm

ROAD

ASHBY

6

SHBY   ROAD   ASHBY

SERVICES

HYAMS LA   A42

E   F   G   H

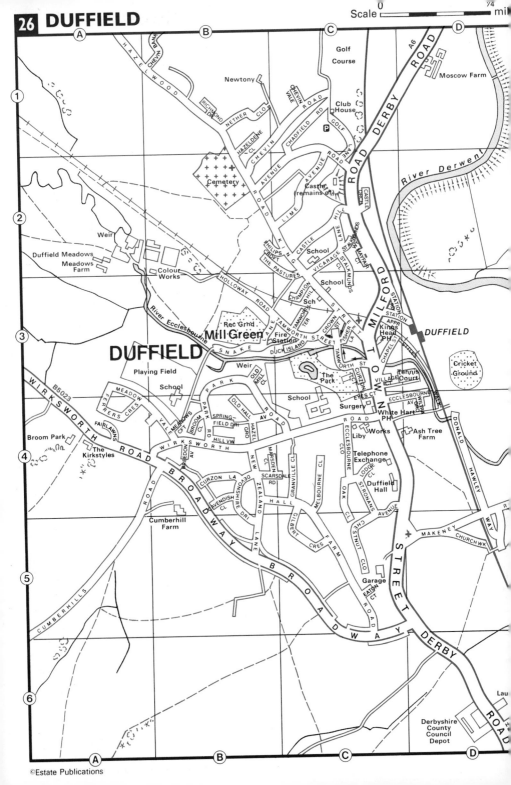

Scale 0 ¼ mi

A B C D

1

Golf Course

Moscow Farm

Newtony

Club House

Cemetery

Castle (remains of)

A6 DERBY ROAD

River Derwent

2

Weir

Duffield Meadows

Meadows Farm

Colour Works

School

School

School Sch

MILFORD ROAD

STATION

3

Rec Grnd

Mill Green

Fire Station

Duck Island

CROWN ST

Kings Head PH

DUFFIELD

DUFFIELD

Playing Field

School

Weir

The Park

Tennis Court

Cricket Ground

The Park

Broom Park

The Kirkstyles

SPRING-FIELD DRI

Surgery

White Hart PH

School

WIRKSWORTH ROAD

B5023

4

Cumberhill Farm

BROADWAY

Works

Liby

Telephone Exchange

Ash Tree Farm

Duffield Hall

DONALD HAWLEY WAY

MAKENEY CHURCH WK

STREET

5

Garage

Derbyshire County Council Depot

Lau

DERBY ROAD

CUMBERHILLS

6

A B C D

©Estate Publications

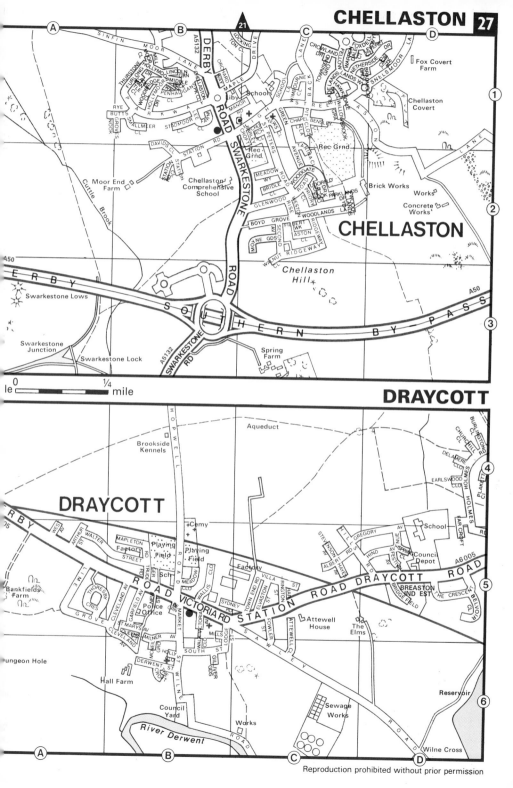

CHELLASTON

DRAYCOTT

DRAYCOTT

The Index includes some names for which there is insufficient space on the maps. These names are preceded by an * and are followed by the nearest adjoining thoroughfare.

DERBY

Abbey Hill. DE22 9 F2
Abbey Hill Rd. DE22 8 D3
Abbey La. DE22 9 F4
Abbey St. DE22 6 B6
Abbey Yd. DE22 9 F4
Abbeyfields Clo. DE22 9 F4
Abbot Clo. DE21 10 B3
*Abbot Mews,
  New Rd. DE22 9 F2
Abbots Barn Clo. DE22 6 B5
Aberdare Clo. DE21 11 F3
Abingdon St. DE24 20 C1
Abney Clo. DE3 12 C5
Acacia Av. DE3 12 B6
Acorn Clo. DE24 21 E5
Acorn Way. DE21 11 F4
Acrefield Way. DE73 21 G6
Acton Rd. DE22 12 D1
Adelphi Clo. DE23 18 D2
Addison Rd. DE24 20 C1
Adelaide Clo. DE3 12 C3
Adelphi Clo. DE23 18 D2
Adler Ct. DE1 6 D1
Adrian St. DE24 29 D2
Agard St. DE1 6 A2
Aimploy Ct. DE23 14 B6
Ainley Clo. DE24 21 F2
Ainsworth Dri. DE23 19 G2
Airedale Walk. DE23 21 H2
Albany Rd. DE22 13 F4
Albemarle Rd. DE21 16 A1
Albert Cres. DE21 15 H3
Albert Rd. DE21 15 G3
Albert St. DE1 6 C4
Albion St. DE1 6 C4
Albrighton Av. DE24 19 F6
Alder Clo. DE21 10 C3
Alder Walk. DE23 6 C6
Alderfen Clo. DE24 20 D5
*Alderly Ct, Winchcombe
  Way. DE21 11 E3
Aldersgate. DE22 12 D1
Aldersley Clo. DE65 16 B4
Aldwick Clo. DE3 12 A5
Aldwych. DE22 13 F1
Alexandra Gdns. DE23 14 C5
Alexandre Clo. DE23 19 G2
Alfreton Rd. DE21 10 A3
Alice St. DE1 6 D2
Alison Clo. DE21 10 D6
All Saints Ct. DE3 12 B6
Allan Av. DE23 18 C1
Allen St. DE24 20 D3
Allestree Clo. DE24 21 E1
Allestree La. DE22 8 D4
Allestree St. DE24 21 E1
Alma Heights. DE3 12 C5
Alma St. DE22 6 A4
Almond St. DE23 14 B5
Alsager Clo. DE21 11 F3
Alstonfield Dri. DE22 9 E4
Alton Clo. DE22 8 D3
Alum Clo. DE24 21 H2
Alvaston St. DE24 21 G1
Alverton Clo. DE3 12 A6
Alwards Clo. DE24 21 F2
Amber Rd. DE22 8 D4
Amber St. DE24 20 C2
Amberley Dri. DE24 19 H3
Ambervale Clo. DE23 18 D3
Ambrose St. DE23 14 B5
Ambrose Ter. DE23 13 H2
Amen Alley. DE1 6 C4
Amesbury La. DE21 10 C4
Amy St. DE22 13 G4
*Anchor Fold,
  Madeley St. DE23 13 H2
Anderson St. DE24 21 F2
Andrew Clo. DE23 18 C1
Anglers La. DE21 16 C4

Anglesey St. DE21 10 B6
Anne Potter Clo. DE72 17 G2
Anstey Ct. DE21 10 D4
Anthony Cres. DE24 21 F3
Anthony Dri. DE24 21 F3
Appian Way. DE24 21 H3
Appleby Dri. DE21 13 H4
Applecross Ct. DE24 19 G5
Appledore Dri. DE21 11 E4
Applegate Clo. DE21 11 E3
Applemead Clo. DE21 10 C4
Appleton Clo. DE21 15 G1
Appletree Clo. DE72 17 G6
Arbor Clo. DE22 6 A5
Arboretum Sq. DE23 14 C4
Arboretum St. DE23 14 C4
Archer St. DE24 15 E5
Arden Clo. DE23 13 G5
Ardleigh Clo. DE3 18 B1
Argyle St. DE22 13 H4
Argyll Clo. DE21 16 D3
Arkendale Walk. DE24 21 H2
Arkle Grn. DE24 19 G4
Arkwright St. DE24 20 C2
Arleston La. DE24 19 G5
Arleston St. DE23 20 A2
Arlington Dri. DE24 21 E3
Arlington Rd. DE23 13 G6
*Armscote Clo, Charingworth
  Rd. DE21 11 E4
Arnhem Ter. DE21 16 C4
Arnold St. DE22 13 G2
Arran Clo. DE24 19 G5
Arreton Ct. DE24 21 H4
Arridge Rd. DE21 15 F1
*Arthur Ct,
  Malcolm St. DE23 14 C5
Arthur Hind Clo. DE22 9 E6
Arthur St. DE1 6 B1
Arundel Av. DE3 12 C5
Arundel Dri. DE21 16 D3
Arundel St. DE22 13 G4
Ascer Croft. DE21 10 C3
Ascot Dri. DE24 20 D2
Ash Clo. DE22 8 D2
Ash Tree Clo. DE21 10 C2
*Ashborne Ct, Uttoxeter
  Old Rd. DE1 13 F1
Ashbrook Av. DE72 17 F5
Ashbrook Clo. DE22 8 C3
Ashby St. DE24 21 E2
Ashcombe Gdns. DE21 11 E4
Ashcroft Clo. DE24 21 E3
Ashe Pl. DE23 13 H6
Ashfield Av. DE21 10 C5
Ashgrove Ct. DE21 11 F4
Ashleigh Dri. DE73 21 F6
Ashley St. DE22 13 F2
Ashlyn Rd. DE21 14 D2
Ashmeadow. DE72 17 F6
Ashopton Av. DE23 19 H1
Ashovers Clo. DE21 10 C5
Ashover Rd,
  Allestree. DE22 8 D4
Ashover Rd,
  Chaddesden. DE21 10 C5
Ashton Clo. DE3 12 A4
Ashtree Av. DE24 20 B2
Ashwater Clo. DE24 19 H6
Ashworth Av. DE21 15 F3
Askerfield Av. DE22 8 C2
Aspen Dri. DE21 16 A3
Asterdale Vw. DE21 16 D3
Aston Rd. DE23 19 F3
Astorville Pk Rd. DE73 21 F5
Atchison Gdns. DE21 16 A1
Atherfield Walk. DE24 21 H3
Athlone Clo. DE21 10 B5
Athol Clo. DE24 21 G6
Atlow Rd. DE21 10 C6
Attlebridge Clo. DE21 10 B5
*Atworth Gro,
  Bridgeness Rd. DE23 18 D2
Auckland Clo. DE3 12 A5
Audrey Dri. DE21 11 E5
Augusta St. DE23 14 C4
Aults Clo. DE65 18 A6
Austen Av. DE23 19 H2
Austin Sq. DE23 19 H2
Autumn Gro. DE21 15 G3
Averham Clo. DE21 11 E5

Aviemore Way. DE24 19 G4
Avocet Clo. DE24 19 G5
Avon Clo. DE24 19 G6
Avon St. DE24 15 F6
Avondale Rd,
  Derby. DE23 6 B6
Avondale Rd,
  Spondon. DE21 16 C2
Avonmouth Dri. DE24 21 E1
Aycliffe Gdns. DE24 21 E4
Aylesbury Av. DE21 10 C6
Ayre Clo. DE21 16 C3

Babbacombe Clo. DE24 21 H2
Babington La. DE1 6 C5
Back La. DE73 21 F6
Back Sitwell St. DE1 6 C5
Badger Clo. DE21 16 D1
Bagshaw St. DE24 21 E1
Bailey St. DE23 14 B5
Bainbrigge St. DE23 14 B5
Bains Dri. DE72 17 G6
Bakeacre La. DE65 18 B6
Bakehouse La. DE72 17 F5
Baker St. DE24 21 E1
Bakers La. DE1 6 B5
Bakewell Clo. DE3 12 B4
Bakewell St. DE22 6 A4
Balaclava Rd. DE23 20 A1
Balfour Rd. DE23 20 A1
Balham Walk. DE22 12 D1
Ballards Way. DE72 17 G6
Ballater Clo. DE24 19 H4
Balleny Clo. DE21 10 C4
Balmoral Clo. DE23 13 E5
Balmoral Rd. DE72 17 F6
*Balness Ct, Tobermory
  Way. DE24 19 G5
Bamburgh Clo. DE21 16 C3
Bamford Av. DE23 19 H1
Bancroft Dri. DE22 8 D2
Bangor St. DE21 10 C6
Bank Croft. DE22 9 E6
Bank Side. DE22 9 E4
Bank View Rd. DE22 9 F5
Bankfield Dri. DE21 16 D3
Bankholmes Clo. DE24 19 G6
Bannels Av. DE23 12 A4
Banwell Clo. DE23 12 A4
*Barcheston Clo, Charingworth
  Rd. DE21 11 E4
Barden Dri. DE22 9 F3
*Bardsey Ct,
  Holyhead Dri. DE21 11 E3
Bare La. DE21 17 F3
Barf Clo. DE3 12 C6
Barleycorn Clo. DE21 16 D1
Barlow St. DE1 14 D4
Barn Clo. DE65 18 B5
Barnard Rd. DE21 10 B4
Barnes Grn. DE22 13 E1
Barnhill Gro. DE23 18 D2
*Barnstaple Clo, Countisbury
  Dri. DE24 10 D4
Barnwood Clo. DE3 12 A5
Baron Clo. DE21 11 G3
Barrett St. DE24 21 F2
Barrie Dri. DE24 20 A4
Barrons Way. DE72 17 F6
Barton Clo. DE21 16 D2
Basildon Clo. DE24 21 E4
Baslow Dri. DE22 9 F3
Bass St. DE22 13 F2
Bassingham Clo. DE21 11 E4
Bateman St. DE23 14 D5
Bath Rd. DE3 12 C5
Bath St. DE1 6 C1
Baverstock Clo. DE73 21 F5
Baxter Sq. DE23 19 H2
Bayleaf Cres. DE21 11 E3
Bayswater Clo. DE22 12 D2
Beardmore Clo. DE21 10 C4
Beatty St. DE24 21 E1
Beaufort Rd. DE24 19 F6
Beaufort St. DE21 10 B5
Beaumaris Ct. DE21 16 D2
Beaumont Walk. DE23 19 H2
Beaureper Av. DE22 8 D3
Becher St. DE23 14 C6
Beckenham Way. DE22 13 E1
Becket St. DE1 6 B4
Becket Well La. DE1 6 B4

Beckitt Clo. DE24 21 F1
Bedford Clo. DE22 13 G4
Bedford St. DE22 13 G3
Beech Av,
  Alvaston. DE24 21 G1
Beech Av,
  Borrowash. DE72 17 F4
Beech Ct. DE21 16 C3
Beech Croft. DE21 10 B2
Beech Delve. DE65 18 B6
Beech Dri. DE22 9 F5
Beech Gdns. DE24 21 G1
Beech Walk. DE23 13 G6
Beeches Av. DE23 16 B3
Beechley Dri. DE21 11 E4
Beechwood Cres. DE23 13 F6
Beeley Clo,
  Allestree. DE22 8 D4
Beeley Clo,
  Chaddesden. DE21 10 D4
Belfast Walk. DE21 15 H3
Belfry Clo. DE3 14 B4
Belgrave St. DE23 14 B4
Bellingham Ct. DE22 8 C4
Belmont Dri. ED72 17 F5
Belmont Rd. DE3 12 B3
Belper Rd. DE1 9 F6
Belsize Clo. DE22 12 D2
Belvedere Clo. DE3 12 B4
Belvoir St. DE23 14 A5
Bembridge Dri. DE21 21 H3
Bemrose Mews. DE22 13 F4
Bemrose Rd. DE24 20 D2
Bendall Grn. DE23 19 F3
Benmore Ct. DE21 11 E3
Bennett St. DE24 20 D3
Benson St. DE24 21 E2
Bentley St. DE24 21 E2
Beresford Dri. DE21 16 D4
Berkley Clo. DE23 19 G1
Berkshire St. DE21 10 B6
Berry Farm Ct. DE24 9 E4
Berrysford Clo. DE21 15 F3
Berwick Av. DE21 10 B6
Berwick Ct. DE21 21 G4
Berwick Dri. DE24 19 F5
Besthorpe Clo. DE21 11 E5
*Betjeman Sq, Wordsworth
  Dri. DE24 20 A3
Bethulie Rd. DE23 20 A1
Beverley St. DE24 15 E5
Bewdley Clo. DE73 21 F5
Bexhill Walk. DE21 10 B4
Bicester Av. DE24 19 F6
*Bickley Moss,
  Rosemoor La. DE21 11 E4
Bideford Dri. DE23 19 G3
Bingham St. DE24 20 D3
Binscombe La. DE21 10 C3
Birch Clo. DE22 17 E2
Birch View Ct. DE1 6 A1
Birches Rd. DE22 8 D2
Birchfield Clo. DE21 21 F6
Birchover Rise. DE21 10 D4
Birchover Way. DE22 8 D4
Birchwood Av. DE72 19 F3
Birdcage Walk. DE22 12 D2
Birdwood St. DE23 14 A6
Birkdale Clo. DE3 12 D5
Biscay Ct. DE21 11 F3
Bishops Dri. DE23 19 G3
Blaby Clo. DE3 19 H2
Blackmore St. DE23 19 G5
Blackmount Ct. DE24 10 C3
Blackthorn Clo. DE21 10 C3
Blagreaves Av. DE23 19 F3
Blagreaves La. DE23 19 F1
Blakebrook Dri. DE73 21 F5
Blakeney Ct. DE21 11 F4
Blandford Clo. DE24 21 H3
Blankney Clo. DE24 19 G6
Blencathra Dri. DE22 12 C6
Blenheim Dri. DE22 8 D2
Blithfield Gdns. DE73 21 F6
Bloomfield Clo. DE1 14 C4
Bloomfield St. DE1 14 D4
Bluebell Clo. DE24 19 F6
Bluebird Clo. DE24 19 G4
Blyth Pl. DE21 10 B4
Boden St. DE23 14 C5
Bodmin Clo. DE24 21 G3
Bodmin Grn. DE24 21 G3

Bold La. DE1 6 B
Bonchurch Clo. DE24 21 H
Bonnyrigg Dri. DE21 10 D
Bonsall Av. DE23 13 G
Bonsall Dri. DE3 12 B
Booth St. DE24 21 E
Border Cres. DE24 21 G
Borrow Fields. DE72 17 F
Borrowash. DE72 16 C3
Borrowash By-Pass.
  DE21 16 C
Borrowash Rd. DE21 16 D
Borrowfield Rd. DE21 16 C
Boscastle Clo. DE24 21 G
Boston Clo. DE21 16 B
Boswell Sq. DE23 19 H
Bosworth Av. DE23 19 G
Boulton Dri. DE24 21 H
Boulton La. DE24 21 H
Boundary Rd. DE22 13 C
Bourne St. DE1 6 C
Bowbank Clo. DE23 18 D
Bowbridge Av. DE23 19 H
Bower St. DE24 21 H
Bowland Clo. DE3 12 C
Bowlees Ct. DE23 18 C
Bowmer Rd. DE23 15 H
Boxmore Clo. DE23 18 E
Boyer St. DE22 6 A
*Boyer Walk,
  Boyer St. DE22 6 A
Boylestone Rd. DE23 19
Brackens Av. DE24
Brackens La. DE24
Brackensdale Av. DE22 13
Brackley Dri. DE21 16
Bracknell Dri. DE24
Bradbourne Ct. DE22 13
Bradbury Dri. DE72
Bradgate Ct. DE23 19
Brading Clo. DE24 21
Bradley St. DE22 9
Bradmoor Gro. DE73
Bradshaw Way. DE1 6
Bradwell Clo. DE3
Braemar Clo. DE24 19
Brailsford Rd. DE21 10
Braintree Clo. DE21 10
Braithwell Clo. DE24 9
Bramble St. DE1
Bramblewick Dri. DE24
*Brambleberry Ct, Cherrybr
  Dri. DE24 11
Bramfield Av. DE22 13
Bramley Clo. DE21 1
Brampton Clo. DE3 12
Brandelhow Ct. DE21
Branksome Av. DE24 21
Brassington Rd. DE21 10
Brayfield Av. DE23 19
Brayfield Rd. DE23 19
Brecon Clo. DE21 16
Breedon Av. DE23 18
Breedon Hill Rd. DE23 14
Bretby Sq. DE23 18
Bretton Av. DE23 1
Breydon Clo. DE24 20
Briar Clo,
  Borrowash. DE72 1
Briar Clo,
  Chaddesden. DE21 16
Briar Lea Clo. DE24 20
Briars Gate. DE22 8
Briars La. DE22
Briarwood Way. DE23 1
Brick Row. DE22
Bridge Gate. DE1
Bridge St. DE1
*Bridgend Ct, Leominster
Bridgeness Rd. DE23 1
Bridgeport Rd. DE21 1
Bridgwater Clo. DE21 1
Brierfield Way. DE3 1
Brigden Av. DE24 1
Brighstone Clo. DE24 1
Bright St. DE22 1
Brighton Rd. DE24 2
Brigmor Walk. DE22
Brindley Clo. DE24

3rindley Ct,
Evans St. DE24 21 E2
'isbane Rd. DE3 12 C4
'iset Clo. DE24 19 G6
'istol Dri. DE3 12 C5
'itannia Ct. DE1 6 C1
'oadbank. DE22 8 D6
'oadfields Clo. DE22 9 E5
3roadleaf Clo, Spindletree
Dri. DE21 10 C4
'oadway Park Clo.
DE22 9 E5
'oadstone Clo. DE21 10 D5
'oadway. DE22 9 E5
'ockley. DE21 16 C2
'omley St. DE22 9 E6
'ompton Rd. DE22 12 D2
'omyard Dri. DE73 21 F5
'onte Pl. DE23 19 E1
rook Clo,
Burley La. DE22 8 C2
rook Clo,
Findern. DE65 18 B6
'ook Gdns. DE22 6 A1
'ook Rd. DE72 17 F6
'ook St. DE1 6 A2
'ook Walk. DE1 6 A2
'ookfield Av,
Chaddesden. DE21 11 E6
'ookfield Av,
Sunny Hill. DE23 19 G2
'ookfields Dri. DE21 10 B2
'ookhouse St. DE24 20 D3
'ooklands Dri. DE23 19 F1
'ookside Clo. DE22 13 G1
'ookside Rd. DE21 10 B2
'oom Clo,
Chellaston. DE73 21 E6
'oom Clo,
Sinfin. DE24 19 G6
'oomhill Clo. DE3 12 B4
'ough St. DE22 13 G2
'oughton Av. DE23 13 G6
'owning Circle. DE23 19 H2
'owning St. DE23 19 H1
'unswick St. DE23 14 B6
'unswood Clo. DE21 16 C2
'unton Clo. DE3 12 A6
'yony Clo. DE21 10 D4
ıchan St. DE24 20 D2
ıchanan St. DE1 6 C1
ıckingham Av. DE21 10 B6
ıckland Clo. DE22 13 H2
ıckminster Clo. DE21 10 D3
ıller St. DE23 13 H5
ınting Clo. DE3 13 E4
ırbage Pl. DE24 21 E2
ırdock Clo. DE21 10 C3
ırghley Clo. DE73 21 E6
ırghley Way. DE23 18 C3
ırleigh Dri. DE22 9 F6
ırlington Rd. DE22 12 C2
ırlington Way. DE22 12 B6
ırnaby St. DE24 15 F6
ırnage Ct. DE22 6 A5
ırnham Dri. DE3 12 A5
ırns Clo. DE23 19 E1
ırnside Clo. DE24 19 G5
ırnside Dri. DE21 16 D3
ırnside St. DE24 21 F1
ırrowfield Mews.
DE21 16 D5
ırrows Walk. DE1 6 C4
ırton Rd, Derby. DE1 6 A6
ırton Rd,
Findern. DE65 18 A6
ırton Rd,
Littleover. DE23 13 E6
ıte Walk. DE21 10 B6
ıttermere Dri. DE22 9 E2
ıtterwick Clo. DE23 19 H3
ıttonoak Dri. DE73 21 F5
ıxton Dri. DE21 12 C4
ıxton Rd. DE21 10 D5
/field Clo. DE21 11 E3
/ng Av. DE23 20 A1
/ron St. DE23 14 B5

ıdgwith Dri. DE22 9 E3
ıdwell Clo. DE24 21 H3
ıerhays. DE24 19 G5
ıernarvon Clo. DE21 16 D2
ıesar St. DE1 9 G6
ıirngorm Dri. DE24 19 G5
ıirns Clo. DE3 12 C4
ılder Clo. DE22 9 E3
ıldermill Dri. DE21 10 D4
ılifornia Gdns. DE22 13 F4
'llow Hill Way. DE23 18 D2
Calver Clo. DE21 10 C3
Calvert St. DE1 14 D4
Calverton Clo. DE24 21 E5
Calvin Clo. DE24 21 F4
Camberwell Av. DE22 13 E2
Camborne Clo. DE21 10 C5
Cambridge St,
Derby. DE23 14 C5
Cambridge St,
Spondon. DE21 16 C4
Camden St. DE22 13 G3
Camellia Clo. DE3 12 B4
Cameron St. DE23 14 B6
Camp St. DE1 9 G6
Campbell St. DE24 20 D2
Campion St. DE22 13 G2
*Campsie Ct, Tobermory
Way. DE24 19 G5
Canal St. DE1 14 C4
Canberra Clo. DE3 12 C5
Canons Walk. DE22 9 F4
Canterbury St. DE21 10 C5
Cantley Clo. DE24 20 D5
Cardales Clo. DE65 18 B5
Cardean Clo. DE1 14 C1
Cardigan St. DE21 10 B6
Cardinal Clo. DE21 10 C3
Cardrona Clo. DE21 10 D4
Carisbrooke Gdns. DE23 19 F3
Carlisle Av. DE23 19 E1
Carlton Av. DE24 20 D5
Carlton Dri. DE24 20 D5
Carlton Gdns. DE24 20 D5
Carlton Rd. DE23 13 G6
Carlton Walk. DE24 15 G6
Carlyle St. DE24 20 A3
Carnegie St. DE23 20 B1
Carnforth Clo. DE3 12 C6
Carnoustie Clo. DE3 12 D5
Carol Cres. DE21 15 F3
Caroline Clo. DE24 21 H2
Carrington St. DE1 6 D5
Carron Clo. DE24 19 G4
Carsington Cres. DE22 8 D5
Carsington Mews. DE22 9 E5
Carson Rd. DE21 16 A1
Carter St. DE24 20 D3
Cascade Gro. DE23 18 D1
Casson Av. DE24 21 F2
Castings Rd. DE23 14 C6
Castle Clo. DE72 17 G5
Castle Croft. DE24 21 H4
Castle Hill. DE65 18 B6
Castle Shaw Dri. DE23 18 C2
Castle St. DE1 6 D5
Castle Walk. DE1 6 D4
Castlecraig Ct. DE24 19 G6
Castleton Av. DE23 19 H1
Cathedral Pl. DE1 6 C2
Cathedral Rd. DE1 6 B2
Cathedral Vw. DE22 13 G5
Catherine St. DE23 14 C5
Catterick Dri. DE3 12 A6
Causeway. DE22 9 E3
Cavan Dri. DE21 15 H3
Cavendish Av. DE22 9 E3
Cavendish Ct. DE1 6 B2
Cavendish St. DE1 6 A3
Cavendish Way. DE3 12 C5
Caversfield Clo. DE23 18 D1
Caxton St. DE23 19 G2
Cecil St. DE22 13 G2
Cedar Dri. DE72 17 G3
Cedar St. DE22 9 E4
Cedarwood Clo. DE21 10 C3
Celandine Clo. DE21 10 D4
Celanese Rd. DE21 16 B4
Central Av. DE72 17 F6
Centre Ct. DE1 14 D4
Centurion Walk. DE1 9 G6
Chaddesden La. DE21 15 G2
Chaddesden Lane End.
DE21 15 G2
Chaddesden Park Rd.
DE21 15 F2
Chadwick Av. DE24 21 E3
Chaffinch Clo. DE21 16 D1
Chain La. DE23 13 E6
Chalfont Sq. DE21 11 F4
Chalkley Clo. DE24 21 E1
Challis Av. DE21 15 H1
Chambers St. DE24 15 F6
Chancel Pl. DE22 6 A6
Chancery La. DE22 13 E2
Chandlers Ford. DE21 10 C4
Chandos St. DE22 13 G2
Chandres Ct. DE22 9 E2
Chantry Clo. DE3 12 B6
Chapel La,
Cherrytree Hill. DE21 15 G1
Chapel La, Derby. DE1 14 C4
Chapel La,
Spondon. DE21 16 C2
Chapel Pl. DE1 6 C5
Chapel Row. DE72 17 F5
Chapel St, Derby. DE1 6 B2
Chapel St,
Spondon. DE21 16 C3
*Chapelside,
Strathaven Ct. DE21 16 C3
Chapman Av. DE24 21 G2
Chapter Clo. DE21 10 B3
Charing Ct. DE1 6 D1
Charingworth Rd. DE21 11 E4
Chariot Clo. DE24 21 H3
Charlbury Clo. DE23 18 B1
Charles Av. DE21 16 C2
Charles Rd. DE24 15 G6
Charleston Dri. DE22 8 D2
Charleston Rd. DE21 16 A2
Charlotte St. DE23 14 B5
Charnwood Av,
Borrowash. DE72 17 G5
Charnwood Av,
Littleover. DE23 19 G3
Charnwood St. DE1 6 C6
Charterhouse Clo.
DE21 10 C3
Charterstone La. DE22 9 E2
Chartwell Dri. DE21 14 D2
Chase Clo. DE73 21 G6
Chatham St. DE23 20 A1
Chatsworth Ct. DE24 20 A4
Chatsworth Cres. DE22 9 E3
Chatsworth Dri. DE3 12 C5
Chatsworth St. DE23 14 A6
Chatteris Dri. DE21 10 B6
Cheadle Clo. DE23 13 E6
Cheam Clo. DE22 12 C2
Cheapside. DE1 6 B3
Chedworth Dri. DE24 21 H3
Chellaston Rd. DE24 20 D3
Chelmarsh Clo. DE72 21 F5
Chelmorton Pl. DE21 10 D5
Chelmsford Clo. DE3 12 B4
Chelsea Clo. DE22 12 C2
Chelwood Rd. DE73 21 E6
Chequers La. DE21 15 E2
Chequers Rd. DE21 15 E2
Cheriton Gdns. DE23 18 C2
Cherry Tree Mews.
DE21 16 A3
Cherrybrook Dri. DE21 11 E3
Chertsey Rd. DE3 12 A5
Chesapeake Rd. DE21 16 A2
Cheshire St. DE24 20 D3
Chester Av. DE22 9 G1
Chester Ct. DE21 16 C4
Chester Green Rd. DE1 9 G6
Chesterford Ct. DE23 18 C2
Chesterton Av. DE23 19 G2
Chesterton Rd. DE21 16 D2
Chestnut Av,
Chellaston. DE73 21 E5
Chestnut Av,
Derby. DE23 14 B5
Chestnut Av,
Mickleover. DE3 12 B4
Chestnut Gro. DE72 17 F4
Cheveley Ct. DE21 10 B5
Cheverton Clo. DE24 21 H4
Chevin Av,
Borrowash. DE72 17 F5
Chevin Av,
Mickleover. DE3 12 D5
Chevin Pl. DE1 9 F6
Chevin Rd. DE1 9 F6
Cheviot St. DE22 13 F2
Cheyenne Gdns. DE21 16 A2
Cheyne Walk. DE22 13 F1
Chilston Dri. DE3 12 A4
Chime Clo. DE21 10 C4
Chingford Ct. DE22 13 E2
Chinley Rd. DE21 10 D5
Chiswick Clo. DE22 12 D2
*Christchurch Ct,
St Michaels La. DE1 6 C2
Church Hill. DE21 16 C3
Church Hill Ter. DE21 16 C3
Church La,
Allestree. DE22 9 F3
Church La,
Breadsall. DE21 10 B2
Church La,
Cherrytree Hill. DE21 15 G1
Church La,
Markeaton. DE22 8 A6
Church Lane Nth. DE22 9 F3
Church Mews. DE21 16 C3
Church Rd. DE22 8 C2
Church St,
Alvaston. DE24 21 H2
Church St,
Derby. DE23 14 B5
Church St,
Littleover. DE23 13 F6
Church St,
Ockbrook. DE72 17 G3
Church St,
Spondon. DE21 16 C3
Church Walk. DE22 9 F2
Churchdown Clo. DE21 11 E3
Churchside Walk. DE22 13 G4
City Rd. DE1 6 C1
Clarence Rd. DE23 14 A6
Clarke St. DE1 6 D1
Cleveland Av. DE21 15 H3
Clifford St. DE24 15 E5
Clifton Dri. DE3 12 C4
Clifton Rd. DE22 8 D3
Clifton St. DE1 14 D4
Clinton St. DE21 15 E2
Clipstone Gdns. DE21 11 F4
Clock Way. DE21 16 D4
*Clock Yard,
Vernon St. DE1 13 H2
Cloisters Ct. DE21 10 D3
Cloudwood Clo. DE23 13 E6
Clover Clo. DE21 16 D3
Cloverdale Dri. DE24 19 H6
Cloverslade. DE65 18 A6
Clumber Ter. DE1 15 E5
Cobden St. DE22 13 G2
Cobham Clo. DE24 19 F5
Cobthorn Dri. DE22 8 D2
Coburn Pl. DE1 6 B3
Cockayne St Nth. DE24 21 E2
Cockayne St Sth. DE24 21 E3
Codbeck Clo. DE24 21 H2
Coke St. DE22 13 G3
Coldstream Walk. DE24 19 G4
Cole La. DE72 17 G4
Coleman St. DE24 21 E2
Coleraine Clo. DE21 15 H3
Coleridge St. DE23 19 H3
College Mews. DE1 13 G3
College Pl. DE1 6 C2
Collier La. DE72 17 F4
Collingham Gdns. DE22 12 D2
Collis Clo. DE24 21 E2
Collumbell Av. DE72 17 G2
Colombo St. DE23 14 C6
Coltsfoot Dri. DE24 19 H6
Columbine Clo. DE21 10 D4
Colvile St. DE22 13 G2
Colwell Dri. DE24 21 H4
Colwyn Av. DE23 13 G6
Colyear St. DE1 6 B4
Comfrey Clo. DE23 18 D2
Commerce St. DE24 15 F6
Common Piece La.
DE65 18 B6
Compton Clo. DE24 21 H3
Coniston Av. DE21 16 C2
Coniston Cres. DE21 10 B4
Connaught Rd. DE22 13 F4
Consett Clo. DE21 10 B5
Consort Gdns. DE21 11 F2
Constable Av. DE23 13 F5
Constable Dri. DE23 13 F5
Constable La. DE23 13 F5
Conway Av. DE72 17 G5
Cookham Clo. DE3 12 A5
Cooper St. DE22 13 F2
Cooperative St. DE23 14 B5
Coopers Clo. DE72 17 G6
*Cope Clo, Wordsworth
Dri. DE24 20 A3
Copecastle Sq. DE1 6 D4
Copeland St. DE1 6 D4
Copes Way. DE21 11 E5
Copperleaf Clo. DE22 6 A5
Coppice Clo. DE22 9 F4
Coppicewood Dri. DE23 12 D6
Copse Gro. DE23 18 D2
Corbel Clo. DE21 10 B4
Corbridge Gro. DE23 18 D2
Corby Clo. DE24 21 F3
Corden Av. DE3 12 D5
Corden St. DE23 14 B5
Cordville Clo. DE21 16 A3
Corfe Clo. DE23 19 G2
Coriander Gdns. DE23 19 F4
Corinium Clo. DE24 21 H3
Corn Market. DE1 6 C3
Cornflower Dri. DE21 11 E3
Cornhill. DE22 9 E2
Cornwall Rd. DE21 15 E1
Coronation Av. DE24 21 G3
Coronation St. DE23 14 C6
Coronet Ct. DE21 11 G3
Corporation St. DE1 6 C3
Cotswold Clo. DE23 19 F1
Cottisford Clo. DE23 19 E1
Cotton Brook Rd. DE23 14 C6
Cotton La. DE24 14 D6
Countisbury Dri. DE21 10 D4
Courtland Dri. DE24 21 G2
Courtland Gdns. DE24 21 G2
Coverdale Walk. DE24 21 H2
Cowdray Clo. DE24 19 G6
Cowley St. DE1 13 H1
Cowper St. DE24 20 B3
Cowsley Rd. DE21 10 B6
Coxgreen Ct. DE23 18 D2
Coxon St. DE21 16 C2
Crabtree Clo. DE22 8 C2
Crabtree Hill. DE21 8 C2
Craddock Av. DE21 16 C4
Craiglee Ct. DE24 19 G5
Cranberry Gro. DE23 18 D2
Cranhill Dri. DE23 18 C2
Cranmer Rd. DE21 14 D2
Cranwood Clo. DE24 20 D4
Crawley Rd. DE24 21 F3
Crayford Rd. DE24 21 F3
Crecy Clo. DE22 13 F4
*Cressbrook Way,
Smalley Dri. DE21 11 E3
Crew St. DE23 14 B6
Crewton Way. DE24 21 E2
Crich Av. DE23 13 F5
Crich Circle. DE23 13 F5
*Cricketers Ct, Taverners
Cres. DE23 19 F1
Cricklewood Rd. DE22 13 E1
Cringle Mews. DE21 10 C4
Croft Clo,
Ockbrook. DE72 17 F3
Croft Clo,
Spondon. DE21 16 D2
Croft La. DE21 10 B3
*Crofters Ct,
Dunsmore Dri. DE21 10 C4
Cromarty Clo. DE24 19 G4
Cromer Clo. DE3 12 A6
Cromford Dri. DE3 12 B4
Cromford Rd. DE21 10 D6
Crompton St. DE1 6 B4
Cromwell Av. DE65 18 B6
Cromwell Rd. DE23 14 B5
Cropton Clo. DE24 21 H2
Crosby St. DE22 13 G4
Cross Clo. DE23 19 F1
Cross Close Wk. DE23 19 F1
Cross St. DE22 13 G2
Crossdale Gro. DE21 11 F3
Crown Mews. DE22 13 H4
Crown St. DE22 6 A6
Crown Walk. DE1 6 C4
Crowshaw St. DE24 20 C1
Croydon Walk. DE22 12 D1
Cubley Walk. DE23 19 F3
Cuckmere Clo. DE22 9 G1
Cullen Way. DE24 19 H6
*Culworth Ct, Charingworth
Rd. DE21 11 E4
Cumberland Av. DE21 15 E1
Cumberland Cres. DE72 17 E5
Cumbria Walk. DE3 12 A6
Cummings St. DE23 14 B5
Curborough Dri. DE24 21 H3
Curlew Clo. DE24 19 G4
Curzon Clo. DE22 8 C2
Curzon Ct. DE3 12 B6
Curzon La. DE24 21 F1
Curzon Rd. DE21 10 D6
Curzon St. DE1 6 A4
Cut La. DE22 9 G6
Cuttlebrook Clo. DE23 19 G2
Cypress Walk. DE21 16 A3

Dahlia Dri. DE21 11 F3
Dairy House Rd. DE23 14 C6
Dalbury Walk. DE23 19 F3
Dale Rd. DE24 21 G2
Dale Rd. DE23 14 B5
Dale Rd. DE21 16 D2
Dalesgate Clo. DE23 19 E4
Dalkeith Av. DE24 21 E3
Dalton Av. DE22 13 F4
Danebridge Cres. DE21 11 E4
Darby St. DE23 14 B5
Darley Abbey Dri. DE22 9 F4
Darley Gro. DE22 9 F5

Darley La. DE1 6 B1
Darley Park Dri. DE22 9 F5
Darley Park Rd. DE22 9 F5
Darley St. DE22 9 F4
Dartford Pl. DE24 21 F3
Darwin Av. DE24 20 D4
Darwin Pl. DE1 6 D3
Darwin Rd. DE3 12 C4
Darwin Sq. DE1 6 C4
Dashwood St. DE23 14 B4
Datchet Clo. DE23 19 E1
Davenport Rd. DE24 20 C1
Daventry Clo. DE3 12 A4
Dawlish Ct. DE24 21 H1
Dawsmere Clo. DE21 10 B5
Daylesford Clo. DE23 18 D1
Dayton Clo. DE21 16 A2
Deacon Clo. DE21 10 C3
Deadmans La. DE24 15 E5
Dean Clo. DE23 13 E5
Dean St. DE22 13 G4
Deans Dri. DE72 17 F5
Deborah Dri. DE21 11 E6
Dee Clo. DE24 19 G5
Deep Dale La. DE24 19 H6
Deepdale Av. DE72 17 G5
Deepdale Rd. DE21 16 D4
Deer Park View. DE21 16 D1
Degge St. DE1 6 C4
Dein Court Clo. DE21 17 E2
Delamere Clo. DE21 11 E5
Denarth Av. DE24 20 D5
Denbigh St. DE1 10 C6
Denison Gdns. DE21 16 A2
Dennis Clo. DE23 18 C1
Denstone Dri. DE24 21 F4
Dentdale Ct. DE24 21 H2
Denver Rd. DE3 12 B4
Depot St. DE23 14 C5
Derby La. DE23 19 H1
Derby Rd,
 Borrowash. DE72 17 E5
Derby Rd,
 Chaddesden. DE21 11 G3
Derby Rd,
 Chellaston. DE73 21 E5
Derby Rd,
 Cherrytree Hill. DE21 15 G3
Derrington Leys. DE24 21 H2
Derventio Clo. DE1 9 G6
Derwent Av,
 Allestree. DE22 9 F2
Derwent Av,
 Borrowash. DE72 17 G5
Derwent Clo. DE22 9 G2
Derwent Dri. DE24 19 G6
Derwent Par. DE24 15 E4
Derwent Park. DE1 14 D4
Derwent Rise. DE21 16 D3
Derwent Rd. DE21 16 B4
Derwent St. DE1 6 C3
Devas Gdns. DE21 16 B2
Devon Clo. DE21 15 E1
Devonshire Av,
 Allestree. DE22 9 E3
Devonshire Av,
 Borrowash. DE72 17 G5
Devonshire Dri. DE3 12 C5
Devonshire Walk. DE1 6 C4
Dewchurch Dri. DE23 19 G4
Dexter St. DE23 14 D5
Diamond Dri. DE21 10 D3
Dickens Sq. DE23 19 H2
Dickinson St. DE24 15 E5
Diseworth Clo. DE73 21 F6
Dodburn Ct. DE24 19 G4
Doles La. DE65 18 A5
Dolphin Clo. DE21 17 E1
Donegal Walk. DE21 15 H3
Donington Clo. DE23 19 G3
Donington Dri. DE23 19 G3
Dorchester Av. DE21 10 C6
Dorking Rd. DE22 13 E2
Dorrien Av. DE23 20 A1
Dorset St. DE21 15 E1
Douglas St. DE23 14 C5
Dove Clo. DE3 12 D4
Dovecote Dri. DE72 17 E5
Dovedale Av. DE24 21 H2
Dovedale Rise. DE22 8 D5
Dovedale Rd. DE21 16 D4
Dover Ct. DE23 14 B5
Dover St. DE23 14 B6
Doveridge Walk. DE3 19 F3
Dower Clo. DE22 9 F4
Downham Ct. DE3 12 C6
Downing Clo. DE22 12 D2
Downing Rd. DE21 15 E3
Drage St. DE1 9 G6

Draycott Dri. DE3 12 A4
Draycott Rd. DE72 17 G6
Drayton Av. DE22 12 D1
Dresden Clo. DE3 12 A5
Drewry Ct. DE22 13 H3
Drewry La. DE22 6 A4
Dreyfus Clo. DE21 16 D2
Drury Av. DE21 16 C4
Dryden St. DE23 19 H2
Drysdale Rd. DE3 12 B4
Duesbury Clo. DE24 20 D2
Duffield Rd,
 Allestree. DE22 9 F2
Duffield Rd,
 Derby. DE1 6 B1
Duke St. DE1 6 C1
Dukeries La. DE24 11 E4
Duluth Av. DE21 15 H1
Dulverton Av. DE24 19 F6
Dulwich Rd. DE22 12 C2
Dunbar Clo. DE24 19 H6
Duncan Rd. DE23 20 A1
Dunedin Clo. DE3 12 C4
*Dunkery Ct, Countisbury
 Dri. DE21 10 D4
Dunkirk. DE22 6 A4
Dunoon Clo. DE24 19 G5
Dunsmore Dri. DE21 10 C4
Dunstall Park Rd. DE24 20 D1
Dunton Clo. DE21 14 D3
*Dunvegan Clo,
 Lundie Clo. DE24 19 G6
Durham Av. DE21 15 F2
Durley Clo. DE24 21 H2

Elmtree Av. DE24 20 B2
Elmwood Dri. DE21 10 B4
Elton Rd. DE24 20 B1
Elvaston La. DE24 21 G2
Embankment Clo. DE22 12 D1
Emerald Clo. DE21 10 D3
Emerson Sq. DE23 19 H2
Emmerdale Walk. DE21 10 B4
Empress Rd. DE23 14 A5
Endsleigh Gdns. DE22 12 D1
Enfield Rd. DE22 13 E1
Ennis Clo. DE21 16 A1
Enoch Pine Clo. DE21 16 A3
Epping Clo. DE22 12 C2
Epworth Dri. DE24 21 G4
Eskdale Walk. DE24 21 H3
Essex St. DE21 15 E1
Eton St. DE24 15 E6
Etruria Gdns. DE1 6 C1
Ettrick Clo. DE24 19 H6
Etwall Rd. DE3 12 A6
Etwall St. DE22 13 G2
Euston Dri. DE1 6 D1
Evans Av. DE22 9 F1
Evans St. DE21 21 E2
Evanston Gdns. DE21 16 A2
Evelyn Gro. DE21 15 G3
Evergreen Clo. DE21 11 E3
Evesham Clo. DE21 10 C4
Excelsior Av. DE24 21 G2
Exchange St. DE1 6 C4
Exeter Pl. DE1 6 D3
Exeter St. DE1 6 D2

Fairbourne Dri. DE3 12 B3
Fairdene Ct. DE23 14 B5
Faire St. DE22 13 H4
Faires Clo. DE72 17 G6
Fairfax Rd. DE23 14 A5
Fairfield Av. DE72 17 F4
Fairfield Rd. DE23 13 G6
Fairford Gdns. DE23 18 D2
Fairisle Clo. DE21 11 F3
Fairview Clo. DE23 18 D1
Fairway Clo. DE22 8 D3
Fairway Cres. DE22 8 D3
Fairwood Dri. DE24 21 H3
Fallow Rd. DE21 16 D2
Falmouth Rd. DE24 21 H4
Far La. DE72 17 G2
Farley Dri. DE23 13 F5
Farley Rd. DE23 13 G5
Farm Dri. DE24 21 F3
Farm St. DE22 6 A5
Farmhouse Rd. DE24 19 G6
Farmlands La. DE23 19 E2
Farnborough Gdns.
 DE22 9 G2
Farncombe La. DE21 10 C3
Farndale Ct. DE24 21 H2
Farndale Rd. DE3 12 A6
Farningham Clo. DE21 16 D2
Farnway. DE22 9 E4
Farnworth Rd. DE3 12 B5
Farrier Gdns. DE23 18 D2
Farringdon Clo. DE22 12 C2
Faversham Clo. DE24 21 F3
Fellside. DE21 16 D2
Fenchurch Walk. DE22 13 E1
Fenton Rd. DE3 12 A5
Fenwick St. DE22 20 D2
Fernhill Ct. DE73 21 F5
Ferneliffe Gdns. DE21 10 D4
Fernwood Clo. DE3 13 F6
Ferrers Way. DE22 9 E4
Field Clo. DE72 17 F4
Field Cres. DE24 21 F3
Field Dri. DE24 21 G4
Field La,
 Alvaston. DE24 21 G3
Field La,
 Chaddesden. DE21 10 D6
Field Rise. DE23 19 F1
Field View Clo. DE24 21 G4
Fieldare Ct. DE23 18 D2
Fieldgate Dri. DE21 11 E3
Fieldhead Way. DE21 11 E4
Fieldsway Dri. DE21 10 B4
Fife St. DE24 15 F6
Filey Walk. DE21 10 B5
Finch Cres. DE3 12 D4
Fincham Clo. DE21 10 B5
Finchley Av. DE22 12 D1
Findern Clo. DE21 8 D5
Findern La. DE65 18 A5
Findern St. DE22 13 G2
Finmere Clo. DE23 19 E1
Finningley Dri. DE21 9 E4
Finsbury Av. DE22 13 E2

Finsley Walk. DE23 19 H2
Firs Cres. DE22 9 E2
*Firtree Gro,
 Beechley Dri. DE21 11 E4
Fisher St. DE24 20 D3
Fiskerton Way. DE21 11 E5
Five Lamps. DE22 6 A1
Flamstead St. DE24 20 D2
Flat Sq. DE22 9 F4
Fleet St. DE23 14 C5
Flint St. DE24 20 D3
Flood St. DE72 17 F3
Folkestone Dri. DE24 21 F4
Folly Rd. DE22 9 G4
Ford La. DE22 9 G1
Ford St. DE1 6 A3
Fordwells Clo. DE21 11 E3
Fordwells Dri. DE23 19 G1
Forester St. DE1 6 B5
Foresters Way. DE23 6 A4
Forman St. DE1 6 A4
Forum Clo. DE24 21 H3
Fountains Clo. DE22 9 F2
Fowler Av. DE21 16 B3
Fowler St. DE1 13 H2
Fox Clo. DE24 19 F6
Fox St. DE1 6 C1
Foxes Walk. DE22 9 E2
Foxfields Dri. DE21 10 C4
Foxglove Dri. DE21 10 D3
Foxlands Av. DE22 9 E3
Foxley Ct. DE21 16 A3
Foyle Av. DE21 15 G3
*Frampton Gdns, Littlewoodbury
 Dri. DE23 18 D2
*Franchise Ct,
 Franchise St. DE22 13 G3
Franchise St. DE22 13 G3
Francis St. DE21 15 E2
*Frank Dayton Ct,
 Cedar St. DE22 9 E6
Franklyn Dri. DE24 21 F3
Frazer Clo. DE21 16 D2
Frederick Av. DE24 21 G3
Frederick St. DE22 13 G2
Freehold St. DE22 13 G2
Freeman Av. DE23 19 G2
Freemantle Rd. DE3 12 C4
Freesia Clo. DE3 12 C6
French St. DE23 13 G5
Fresco Dri. DE23 18 C2
Friar Gate. DE1 6 A3
Friar Gate Mews. DE1 6 A3
Friars Clo. DE22 9 F3
Friary Av. DE24 21 E3
Friary St. DE1 6 A3
Fritchley Clo. DE21 10 D5
Froggatt Clo. DE22 9 G1
Fulbrook Rd. DE24 19 G1
Fulham Rd. DE22 9 E1
Full St. DE1 6 C2
Fulmar Clo. DE3 12 D4
Furrows Clo. DE21 11 F3

Gable Ct. DE3 12 C6
Gainsborough Clo. DE21 11 E5
Gairloch Clo. DE24 19 H4
Galway Av. DE21 15 H4
Garden St. DE1 6 A1
Garfield Clo. DE23 19 F2
Garrick St. DE24 21 F2
Garry Clo. DE24 19 G6
Garsdale Walk. DE24 21 H2
Garth Cres. DE24 21 G3
Garthorpe Ct. DE21 10 D4
Gary Clo. DE23 19 G3
Gascoigne Dri. DE21 16 B3
Gaskell Av. DE23 19 H2
Gatcombe Clo. DE24 21 E4
Gayton Av. DE23 19 F2
Gayton Thorpe Clo.
 DE23 18 D2
Gemma Clo. DE21 9 G2
George St. DE1 6 B3
George Yd. DE1 6 B3
Gerard Clo. DE1 6 D2
Gerard Ct. DE1 6 B4
Gerard St. DE1 6 A3
Gertrude Rd. DE21 10 D6
Ghyll Clo. DE24 15 G6
Gilbert Clo. DE21 16 C3
Gilbert St. DE24 21 G3
Gilderdale Way. DE21 11 F3
*Gillamore Ct,
 Keldholme La. DE24 21 H2
Gisborne Clo. DE3 12 C4
Gisbourne Cres. DE22 9 F2
Gisbourne Grn. DE1 6 A1

Gladstone Clo. DE73 21
Gladstone Rd. DE21 16
Gladstone St. DE23 13
Glaisdale Nook. DE24 21
Glamis Clo. DE21 11
Glastonbury Rd. DE24 21
Gleadsmoss La. DE21 11
Glebe Rise. DE23 13
Glencroft Dri. DE24 19
Glendale Dri. DE21 16
Glendon Rd. DE24 19
Gleneagles Clo. DE3 12
Glenfield Cres. DE3 12
Glengarry Way. DE24 19
Glenmore Dri. DE24 19
Glenmoy Clo. DE23 19
Glenorchy Ct. DE21 11
Glossop St. DE24 20
Gloster St. DE24 15
Goathland Rd. DE24 19
Goldcrest Dri. DE21 16
Golders Green Wk.
 DE22 12
*Goldstone Ct,
 Gravel La. DE21 16
Golf Clo. DE23 19
Goodale St. DE23 14
Goodrington Rd. DE21 11
Goodsmoor Rd. DE23 19
Goodwood Dri. DE24 21
Gordon Rd,
 Borrowash. DE72 17
Gordon Rd,
 Derby. DE1 6
Gorse Clo. DE23 19
Gorsty Leys. DE65 18
Gosforth Rd. DE24 20
Gower St. DE1 6
Grafham Clo. DE73 21
Grafton St. DE23 13
Grampian Way. DE24 19
Grandstand Rd. DE21 14
Grange Av. DE23 19
Grange Rd. DE24 21
Grange St. DE23 14
Grant Av. DE21 16
Grantham Av. DE21 10
Granville St. DE1 13
Grasmere Av. DE21 16
Grasmere Cres. DE24 16
Grassthorpe Clo. DE21 11
Grassy La. DE23 19
Gravel La. DE1 6
Grayling St. DE23 14
Great Northern Rd. DE1 13
Greatorex Av. DE24 20
Green Acres. DE23 19
Green Bank. DE21 16
Green La,
 Alvaston. DE24 21
Green La, Derby. DE1 6
Green La,
 Ockbrook. DE72 17
Green Park. DE23 12
Greenburn Clo. DE23 19
Greenfields Av. DE23 19
Greenfinch Clo. DE21 16
Greenland Av. DE22 13
Greenmount Clo. DE23 18
Greenside Ct. DE23 12
Greenway. DE65 16
Greenway Clo. DE72 17
Greenway Dri. DE23 13
Greenwich Dri Nth.
 DE22 13
Greenwich Dri Sth.
 DE22 13
Greenwood Av. DE21 10
Greenwood Ct. DE1 6
Gregory Walk. DE23 19
Grenfell Av. DE23 19
Gresham Rd. DE24 19
Grey St. DE1 6
Griffin Clo. DE24 19
Grimshaw Av. DE24 21
Grindlow Rd. DE21 10
Groombridge Cres.
 DE23 18
Grosvenor Dri. DE23 19
Grosvenor St. DE24 20
Grove St. DE23 13
Grovebury Dri. DE23 19
Gurney Av. DE23 19
Gypsy La. DE72 17

Haddon Clo. DE23 8
Haddon Dri,
 Allestree. DE22 9

Haddon Dri, Mickleover. DE3   12 C4
Haddon Dri, Spondon. DE21   16 D4
Haddon St. DE23   14 A5
Haig St. DE24   15 F6
Hailsham Clo. DE3   12 B4
Hains Clo. DE24   20 A4
Halifax Clo. DE21   10 B5
Hall Dyke. DE21   16 C3
Hall Park Clo. DE23   13 E6
Hall St. DE24   21 F1
Hallgate Clo. DE21   11 F3
Halstock Dri. DE24   21 H1
Hambledon Dri. DE24   19 G6
Hamblin Cres. DE24   20 A5
Hamilton Clo. DE3   12 C4
Hamilton Rd, Derby. DE23   14 A5
Hamilton Rd, Spondon. DE21   16 D2
Hampden St. DE23   20 A1
Hampshire Rd. DE21   10 A5
Hampstead Dri. DE22   13 E2
Hampton Clo. DE21   16 D2
Hanbury Rd. DE21   15 F2
Handel St. DE24   14 D6
Handford St. DE22   13 G2
Handyside St. DE1   6 C1
Hanover Sq. DE22   12 D2
Hansard Gate. DE21   14 D2
Hanwell Way. DE24   13 E2
Harcourt St. DE1   6 B5
Hardhurst Rd. DE24   21 G3
Hardwick Av. DE22   8 D2
Hardwick Dri. DE3   12 C5
Hardwick St. DE24   20 C1
Harebell Clo. DE21   10 D3
Harepit Clo. DE24   21 F4
Harewood Rd. DE3   8 D3
Hargrave Av. DE72   17 G2
Hargreaves Clo. DE23   19 E2
Harlech Clo. DE21   17 E2
Harlesden Av. DE22   12 D1
Harlow Clo. DE24   21 E4
Harold Ct. DE23   14 C5
*Harpswell Clo, Finningley Dri. DE22   9 E4
Harpur Av. DE23   13 F4
Harrier Way. DE24   19 G5
Harriet St. DE23   14 C4
Harringay Gdns. DE22   13 F1
Harrington Av. DE72   17 G5
Harrington Rd. DE23   13 F6
Harrington St, Allenton. DE24   21 E3
Harrington St, Pear Tree. DE23   14 C6
Harrison St. DE22   13 H4
Harrow St. DE24   15 E6
Harrogate Cres. DE21   10 B4
Hartington St. DE23   6 C6
Hartington Way. DE3   12 B5
Hartland Dri. DE23   19 G3
Hartshorne Rd. DE23   19 F3
Harvest Way. DE21   11 F3
Harvey Rd. DE24   21 E2
Hasgill Clo. DE21   11 F3
Haslams La. DE22   9 G4
Haslemere Ct. DE23   14 A5
Hassop Rd. DE21   10 D5
Hastings St. DE23   14 B6
Hatchmere Clo. DE21   11 E5
Hatfield Rd. DE24   21 E4
Hathern Clo. DE23   19 G3
Hathersage Av. DE23   19 H1
Havelock Rd. DE23   20 A1
Haven Bank Av. DE23   18 C2
Haven Bank La. DE23   18 B3
Haven Ct, Keldholme La. DE24   21 H2
Hawke St. DE22   13 F2
Hawkshead Av. DE21   10 B4
Hawthorn Av. DE24   21 F2
Hawthorn Cres. DE65   18 B6
Hawthorn St. DE24   20 C1
Hawthorne Av. DE72   17 F4
Hawtrey Gdns. DE21   21 F2
Haydn St. DE1   10 D5
Haydock Park Rd. DE24   21 E1
Hayes Av. DE72   19 G1
Hayfield Gdns. DE23   19 E2
Hazel Av. DE23   19 G2
Hazel Clo. DE65   18 B6
Hazel Dri. DE21   17 E2
Hazelwood Rd. DE23   10 D5
Headingly Clo. DE23   19 F1
Heath Av. DE23   13 F6

Heath Ct. DE24   19 G5
Heath La. DE65   18 B6
Heathcote Clo. DE24   21 G4
Heather Clo. DE24   19 F6
Heather Cres. DE23   19 C2
Heathermead Clo. DE21   10 C4
Hebden Clo. DE24   18 D3
Hebrides Clo. DE24   19 G5
Hedgebank Ct. DE21   11 F3
Hedgerow Gdns. DE21   11 F3
Hedingham Way. DE3   18 B1
Heigham Clo. DE24   20 D5
Helston Clo. DE24   21 G3
Hemlock Clo. DE21   10 D3
Hendon Way. DE24   13 E2
Henley Grn. DE22   12 D2
Henry St. DE1   6 B1
Hereford Rd. DE21   10 B6
Hermitage Av. DE72   17 F5
Hermitage St. DE1   11 F4
Heron Way. DE3   12 D5
Heronswood Dri. DE21   16 C2
Hexham Walk. DE21   10 C4
Heyworth St. DE22   13 F2
Hickling Clo. DE24   20 D5
High St. DE1   14 D4
Highbury Clo. DE22   12 C2
Highfield La. DE21   15 F3
Highfield Mews. DE21   15 F3
Highfield Rd, Derby. DE22   9 E6
Highfield Rd, Littleover. DE23   19 F1
Highfields Gdns. DE22   9 F6
Highgate Dri. DE22   13 E2
Hildegrove Dri. DE73   21 E6
*Hilderstone Clo, Keldolme La. DE24   21 H2
Hill Brow. DE1   6 B5
Hill Clo. DE21   16 C3
Hill Cross Av. DE23   19 F2
Hill Cross Dri. DE23   19 E1
Hill Rise Clo. DE23   19 G1
Hill Top. DE21   10 C3
Hill View Gro. DE21   16 D2
Hillcrest Dri. DE73   21 F5
Hillcrest Rd. DE21   10 B6
Hillcroft Dri. DE72   17 F3
Hillside. DE65   13 E6
Hillside Av. DE21   15 G3
Hillside Cres. DE21   16 D3
Hillside Rd. DE21   16 D3
Hillsway, Littleover. DE23   13 E6
Hillsway, Chellaston. DE73   21 F5
Hilton Clo. DE3   12 B6
Hindscarth Cres. DE3   12 C5
Hobart St. DE3   12 C5
Hobkirk Dri. DE24   19 G5
Hodge Beck. DE24   21 H2
*Hodthorpe Clo, Edwinstowe Rd. DE21   11 E4
Holborn Dri. DE22   12 D1
Holbrook Rd. DE21   21 F3
Holcombe St. DE24   14 C6
Holden Ct. DE24   21 F1
Holderness Clo. DE24   19 G6
Hollies Rd. DE22   8 D2
Hollington Clo. DE21   10 C6
Hollis St. DE24   21 F1
Hollow Wood Av. DE23   19 F1
Holloway Rd. DE21   17 F2
Holly Ct. DE3   12 B6
Hollybrook Way. DE23   13 E6
Holme La. DE21   16 B5
Holmes. DE23   14 B5
Holmfield. DE23   19 H1
*Holmoak Clo, Oakside Way. DE21   11 E3
Holt Av. DE24   21 H3
Holtlands Dri. DE24   21 E3
Holyhead Dri. DE21   11 E3
Holyrood Clo. DE21   16 D2
Home Farm Clo. DE73   17 F2
Home Farm Av. DE22   9 F2
Homesfield Dri. DE61   12 C5
Hope Av. DE5   12 B5
Hopes St. DE1   10 D5
Hopetoun St. DE23   20 B1
Hopton Clo. DE21   10 C3
Hornbeam Clo. DE21   10 C3
Horncastle Rd. DE21   10 B4
Hornsea Rd. DE21   10 B5
Horton St. DE23   14 D5
Horwood Av. DE23   13 G5
Hospital La. DE3   18 A1
*Houghton Ct, Morefern Dri. DE21   10 D4

Hounslow Rd. DE22   13 E2
Houston Clo. DE21   16 A2
Hoveton Clo. DE24   20 D5
Howard St. DE23   14 B5
Howden Clo. DE3   12 A5
Howe St. DE22   13 G2
Howth Clo. DE21   15 G3
Hoylake Clo. DE3   12 A5
Hoylake Dri. DE3   12 A4
Hubertshaw Clo. DE21   11 E3
Hucklow Ct. DE21   11 E3
Hulland St. DE1   14 D4
Hulland Vw. DE22   8 D5
Humber Clo. DE24   21 H3
Humbleton Dri. DE22   13 E2
Hunters Croft. DE24   19 G6
Huntingdon Grn. DE21   14 D2
Huntley Av. DE21   16 D1
Hutton St. DE24   20 D2
Huxley Clo. DE23   19 H2
Hyde Park Rd. DE22   13 E1

Ilford Rd. DE22   12 D2
Ilford Walk. DE21   12 D2
Imperial Ct. DE22   8 D1

INDUSTRIAL & RETAIL:
*Beaufort Ct Ind Est, Mansfield Rd. DE1   9 H5
Carrington Ct Ind Est. DE1   13 H3
Castle Ward Ind Est. DE1   14 C3
Kingsway Ind Est. DE22   13 F3
Kingsway Retail Park. DE22   13 F3
Prime Enterprise Pk. DE1   6 D1
Prime Ind Est. DE24   14 D5
*Racecourse Ind Pk., Mansfield Rd. DE1   9 H5
Raynesway Ind Est. DE24   15 G4
Robinson Ind Est. DE23   14 D5
Stoney Cross Ind Est. DE21   16 C4
The Parker Centre. DE1   19 H1

Industrial St. DE23   14 B5
Ingham Dri. DE3   12 B6
Ingle Clo. DE21   16 C3
Ingleby Av. DE23   19 H1
Inglewood Av. DE3   12 B4
Ingliston Clo. DE24   21 H3
Instow Dri. DE23   19 G3
Inveraray Clo. DE24   19 G5
Iona Clo. DE24   19 H5
Iron Gate. DE1   6 C3
Irvine Clo. DE24   19 G5
Irving Pl. DE24   21 F2
Islay Rd. DE24   19 H4
Isleworth Dri. DE22   12 D2
Ismay Rd. DE21   15 G2
Ivernia Clo. DE23   19 G3
Ivy Ct. DE65   12 B6
Ivy Sq. DE23   14 D5
Ivybridge Clo. DE21   11 F3

Jacksdale Clo. DE22   8 D4
Jackson Av. DE3   12 D5
Jackson St. DE22   13 H3
James Clo. DE1   13 G2
Jarvis Clo. DE24   19 G6
Jarvis Rd. DE24   19 G6
Jasmine Clo. DE21   16 A3
Jedburgh Clo. DE24   19 H5
Jefferson Pl. DE24   21 E2
Jemison Clo. DE24   21 E3
Jessop Dri. DE24   19 G6
*John F. Kennedy Gdns, Ellendale Rd. DE21   16 A1
John Lombe Dri. DE1   6 C1
John St. DE1   14 C3
Johnson Av. DE24   21 F2
Joseph St. DE23   14 B6
Jubalton Clo. DE24   21 E4
Jubilee Rd. DE24   21 E4
Junction St. DE1   13 G3
Jury St. DE1   6 B3

Katrine Walk. DE24   19 G4
Kean Pl. DE24   21 F2
Keats Av. DE23   12 D6
Keble Clo. DE21   14 C4
Kedleston Clo. DE22   8 D4
Kedleston Gdns. DE1   6 A1
Kedleston Rd, Derby. DE22   6 A1

Kedleston Rd, Markeaton. DE22   8 C2
Kedleston St. DE1   6 A1
Kegworth Av. DE21   19 F2
Keldholme La. DE24   21 H2
Kelso Walk. DE24   21 G1
Kelvedon Dri. DE23   18 D2
Kemble Pl. DE24   21 F2
Kempton Park. DE24   20 D1
Kendal Walk. DE21   10 B4
Kendon Av. DE23   19 H2
Kenilworth Av. DE23   20 A1
Kensal Rise. DE22   13 E1
Kensington St. DE1   6 A4
Kent St. DE1   15 E1
Kentish Ct. DE1   6 D1
Kernel Clo. DE23   13 E6
Kerry St. DE21   15 E1
Kershope Dri. DE21   11 E3
Kestrels Croft. DE24   19 G5
Keswick Av. DE21   19 H3
Kevin Clo. DE21   11 E6
Kew Gdns. DE22   13 E2
Keyhaven Clo. DE21   10 B5
Keynsham Clo. DE24   21 E1
Keys St. DE1   6 D2
Kibworth Clo. DE21   11 E5
Kildare St. DE21   15 E1
Killingworth Av. DE24   20 A5
Kilnsey Ct. DE23   18 D3
Kimberley Rd. DE72   17 F5
Kinder Walk. DE21   13 G3
King Alfred St. DE22   6 A5
King St. DE1   6 B1
Kingfisher Ct. DE3   18 A2
Kingfisher Walk. DE21   19 H6
Kings Ct. DE1   6 B1
Kings Croft. DE22   9 F2
Kings Dri. DE23   13 E5
Kings Mead Clo. DE1   6 B1
Kings Mead Walk. DE1   6 A1
Kingsbury Rd. DE22   12 D2
Kingsclere Av. DE21   11 E4
Kingsland Clo. DE21   10 C3
Kingsley Rd. DE22   8 D2
Kingsley St. DE24   20 A3
Kingsmuir Rd. DE3   12 A4
Kingston St. DE1   9 F6
Kingsway. DE22   13 F2
Kingsway Pk Clo. DE22   13 F2
Kinross Av. DE21   10 B6
Kintyre Av. DE24   19 G5
Kipling Dri. DE3   12 B6
Kirk Leys Av N. DE21   16 C4
Kirk Leys Av S. DE21   16 C4
Kirk St. DE1   9 G6
Kirkdale Av. DE21   16 D4
Kirkistown Clo. DE24   21 H3
Kirkland Way. DE24   19 F5
Kirkstead Clo. DE21   11 E5
Kitchener Av. DE23   19 H2
Knights Clo. DE24   19 G6
Knightsbridge. DE22   12 D2
Knoll Clo. DE23   18 D1
Knutsford Grn. DE21   10 B4
Kyle Gro. DE21   11 E3
Kynance Clo. DE24   21 H3

Laburnum Cres. DE22   8 D2
Laburnum Gro. DE21   13 E2
Ladbroke Gdns. DE22   12 D1
Ladybank Rd. DE3   12 A4
Ladybower Rd. DE21   16 D4
Ladycroft Paddock. DE22   9 E2
Ladygrove Cotts. DE22   14 C4
Ladysmith Rd. DE72   17 F5
Lake Dri. DE21   19 H1
Lakeside. DE23   18 D2
*Lambe Ct, Morleston St. DE23   14 C4
Lambley Dri. DE22   8 C4
Lambourne Ct. DE22   9 F2
Lambourne Dri. DE22   9 F2
Lambrook Clo. DE3   12 A5
Lampeter Clo. DE21   11 E4
Lanark St. DE21   10 C6
Lancaster Walk. DE21   14 D2
Lancelot Clo. DE24   19 G5
Lang Rd. DE24   21 F3
Langdale Dri. DE21   10 B4
Langford Rd. DE3   12 B4
Langley Rd. DE21   16 D2
Langley St. DE22   13 G2
Langsett Dri. DE21   21 F6
Lanscombe Park Rd. DE22   9 E4
Lansdowne Av. DE24   21 E4

Lansing Gdns. DE21   16 A2
Lapwing Clo. DE24   19 G6
Larch Clo. DE22   8 D2
Larges St. DE1   13 H2
Lark Clo. DE23   19 F2
Larkhill Cres. DE24   20 A4
*Larkin Clo, Wordsworth Dri. DE24   20 A3
Larkspur Ct. DE21   11 E3
Lashley Gdns. DE21   10 C4
Lathbury Clo. DE21   10 B5
Lathkill Av. DE24   21 H2
Lathkill Rd. DE21   10 D5
Latimer Clo. DE23   18 C2
Latimer St. DE24   20 D2
Latrigg Clo. DE3   12 C6
Lauder Clo. DE24   19 H6
Launceston Rd. DE24   21 G3
Lavender Row. DE22   9 F4
*Laverstoke Ct, Peet St. DE22   13 H3
Lawn Av. DE22   8 D4
Lawn Heads Av. DE23   13 F5
Lawnlea Clo. DE23   19 G3
Lawnside. DE21   16 D2
Lawnswood Clo. DE23   19 F1
Lawrence Av. DE72   11 E6
Lawrence St. DE23   20 A1
Lea Clo, Chaddesden. DE22   9 E3
Lea Clo, Mickleover. DE21   15 F2
Lea Dri. DE3   12 B4
Leacroft Rd. DE23   14 C6
*Leafgreen La, Blagreaves La. DE23   19 F1
Leake St. DE1   13 G2
Leamington Clo. DE23   13 G6
Leander Clo. DE23   19 G1
Leaper St. DE1   13 H1
Leawood Gdns. DE21   11 E3
Ledbury Chase. DE24   19 G6
Ledbury Pl. DE21   10 B4
Leeds Pl. DE1   14 D3
Leeside. DE21   15 G6
Leeway. DE21   16 C4
Leicester St. DE22   13 G4
Leman St. DE21   13 H4
Lens Rd. DE22   8 C3
Lenten Av. DE21   15 F2
Leominster Dri. DE21   11 F3
Leonard St. DE23   6 D6
Leonard Walk. DE23   6 C6
Leopold St. DE1   6 C6
Leslie Clo. DE23   18 C1
Leven Clo. DE24   19 H6
Leveret Clo. DE73   21 G6
Lewis St. DE23   14 A6
Lewiston Rd. DE21   16 A3
Lexington Rd. DE21   16 A3
Leys Field Gdn. DE73   21 F6
Leybrook Clo. DE3   12 B4
Leyland Ct. DE1   9 E6
Leyland St. DE1   13 H1
Leylands. DE22   9 E5
Leytonstone Dri. DE22   12 D2
Lichfield Dri. DE24   21 F1
Lidgate Clo. DE3   12 A6
Lilac Av. DE22   13 E2
Lilac Clo. DE24   21 F3
Lilac Way. DE24   8 D4
Lilian Prime Clo. DE24   21 G1
Lilley St. DE24   21 G3
Lime Av, Breadsall. DE21   10 B4
Lime Av, Derby. DE23   6 B6
Lime Croft. DE22   9 F2
Lime Gro. DE21   15 H3
Lime La. DE21   11 E3
Lime Walk. DE23   13 G6
Limedale Av. DE21   11 E3
Limerick Rd. DE24   15 H3
Limes Av. DE3   12 B6
Limes Ct. DE3   12 B6
Limetree Clo. DE1   6 A3
Linacres Dri. DE73   21 F6
Lincoln Av. DE21   21 F1
Lindford Clo. DE21   10 D3
Lindisfarne Clo. DE24   19 G5
Lindon Dri. DE24   21 H2
Lindrick Clo. DE21   10 D2
Lindsey Clo. DE21   15 E2
Lingfield Rise. DE3   12 A4
Links Clo. DE24   20 A4
Linnet Clo. DE21   16 D1
Linnet Hill. DE3   18 A1
Liskeard Dri. DE22   12 D2

t, Tobermory
...24 19 G4
...er Clo. DE22 13 E4
Lister Clo. DE22 13 E4
Liston Dri. DE22 9 E6
Litchurch La. DE24 14 D5
Litchurch St. DE1 6 D6
Little Bridge St. DE1 6 A2
Little Eaton By-Pass. DE21 10 B1
Little Longstone Clo. DE3 12 C5
Littlemeadow Rd. DE73 21 F6
Little Noel St. DE22 13 G1
Littledale Clo. DE21 11 F3
Littleover Cres. DE23 13 G6
Littleover La. DE23 19 G1
Littlewoodbury Dri. DE23 18 D2
Litton Dri. DE21 16 D4
Liverpool St. DE21 10 C6
Liversage Pl. DE1 6 D5
Liversage Rd. DE1 6 D5
Liversage St. DE1 6 D5
Livingstone Rd. DE23 13 H6
Lloyd St. DE22 13 G2
Lochinvar Clo. DE24 16 D2
Lock Up Yd. DE1 6 C3
Lockington Clo. DE73 21 F6
Locko Ct. DE21 16 C2
Locko Rd. DE21 16 C2
Locomotive Way. DE24 15 E4
Lockwood Rd. DE22 8 D2
Lodge La, Derby. DE1 6 A2
Lodge La, Spondon. DE21 16 C3
Lodge Way. DE3 12 B5
Lombard St. DE22 12 C2
Lomond Av. DE24 19 H6
London Rd, Alvaston. DE24 21 F1
London Rd, Derby. DE1 6 D5
Longbridge La. DE24 20 D1
*Longdons Row, Church St. DE21 16 C3
Longford Clo. DE22 8 D4
Longford St. DE22 13 G2
Longlands La. DE65 18 B6
Longley La. DE21 16 B1
Longstock Clo. DE21 10 C4
Longstone Walk. DE1 6 B6
Longthorpe DE23 18 D2
Lonsdale Pl. DE22 13 G3
Lord St. DE24 20 D3
Lorne St. DE22 13 F2
Lorraine Clo. DE24 21 E5
Loscoe Rd. DE21 10 D5
Lothian Pl. DE21 14 D1
Lothlorien Clo. DE23 19 E2
Loudon St. DE23 14 C5
Louisa Greaves La. DE21 16 C2
Louvain Rd. DE23 13 F4
Lowe St. DE24 20 D2
Lower Dale Rd. DE23 14 A5
Lower Eley St. DE1 6 B5
Lower Green. DE65 18 B6
Lower Rd. DE22 8 A5
Lows Rd. DE73 21 G6
*Loxley Clo, Charingworth Rd. DE21 11 E4
Loxton Clo. DE3 12 B4
Loyne Clo. DE24 19 H6
Luccombe Dri. DE24 21 E5
Lucerne Rd. DE21 11 F3
Ludgate Walk. DE22 12 C2
Ludlow Clo. DE21 16 D3
Lulworth Clo. DE23 19 G2
Lundie Clo. DE24 19 G6
Lupin Clo. DE21 11 F3
Lychgate Clo. DE21 10 B3
Lydstep Clo. DE21 11 F3
Lyndhurst Gro. DE21 15 G3
Lyndhurst St. DE23 14 B5
Lynton St. DE22 13 H3
Lynwood Av. DE21 20 A4
Lytham Clo. DE21 10 B4
Lyttleton St. DE22 13 F2

Macaulay St. DE24 20 A3
Mackenzie St. DE22 13 F2
Macklin St. DE1 6 B4
Mackworth Rd. DE1 13 G1
Macready Pl. DE21 21 F2
Madeley Ct. DE3 12 B4
Madeley St. DE23 14 C5
Madison Av. DE21 10 C6
Maidstone Dri. DE24 21 G3

Main Av. DE22 9 F1
Main Clo. DE24 21 G4
Main St. DE65 18 B6
Maine Dri. DE22 15 G1
Maize Clo. DE23 18 D2
Malcolm Gro. DE23 18 C1
Malcolm St. DE23 14 C5
Malham Rd. DE23 18 D2
Mallard Wk. DE3 18 A1
Maltby Clo. DE21 9 E4
Malton Pl. DE21 10 B5
Malvern Clo. DE24 12 B4
Malvern Way. DE21 10 B5
Manchester St. DE22 13 G2
Manifold Dri. DE24 21 G1
Manor Av. DE23 13 F5
Manor Pk. DE72 17 E6
Manor Park Ct. DE22 13 E4
Manor Park Way. DE22 13 E4
Manor Rd, Borrowash. DE72 17 E6
Manor Rd, California. DE22 13 F4
Mansfield Rd, Derby. DE1 6 C2
Mansfield Rd, Oakwood. DE21 10 C3
Mansfield St. DE1 6 C1
Maple Av. DE23 19 G3
Maple Beck Clo. DE1 6 C1
Maple Dri, Alvaston. DE24 21 F3
Maple Dri, Chellaston. DE73 21 F6
Maple Gro. DE22 8 D1
Mapleton Rd. DE21 10 D5
Marchington Clo. DE22 9 E4
Marcus St. DE1 9 G6
Maree Clo. DE24 19 H5
Marfleet Clo. DE3 12 B4
Margaret Av. DE21 15 F3
Margaret St. DE1 6 B1
Margreave Rd. DE21 11 E3
Marigold Clo. DE21 11 E3
Marina Dri, Allenton. DE24 21 E4
Marina Dri, Spondon. DE21 16 C2
Marjorie Rd. DE21 10 C5
Markeaton La. DE22 8 B6
Markeaton St. DE1 13 G1
Market Pl. DE1 6 C3
Markham Clo. DE21 10 C4
*Markham Ct, Chandlers Ford. DE21 10 C4
Marks Clo. DE23 19 G3
Marlborough Rd. DE24 20 C1
Marsden St. DE24 21 E2
Marshaw Clo. DE3 12 C6
Marshgreen Clo. DE24 21 H4
Marston Clo. DE23 19 F3
Martin Dri. DE21 11 E5
Maryland Rd. DE21 16 A2
Marylebone Cres. DE22 12 D2
Masefield Rd. DE23 19 G2
Masson Wk. DE22 13 H3
Matlock Rd. DE21 10 D4
Matthew St. DE24 21 E3
Matthews Way. DE23 18 C1
Max Rd. DE21 10 C6
Maxwell Av. DE22 8 D5
May St. DE23 6 A6
Mayfair Cres. DE22 12 C2
Mayfield Rd. DE21 10 C6
Maylands. DE22 17 F6
Maypole La. DE23 18 C1
*Mcgough Mews, Wordsworth Dri. DE24 20 A3
Mead Clo. DE24 20 A4
Meadow Clo, Findern. DE65 18 B5
Meadow Clo, Spondon. DE21 16 C3
Meadow La, Alvaston. DE24 15 G6
Meadow La, Cherrytree Hill. DE21 15 G3
Meadownook. DE24 21 H4
Meadow Rd. DE1 6 D3
Meadow View Clo. DE21 11 E3
Meadowgrass Clo. DE23 19 E2
Meadowlark Gro. DE21 10 D4
Mear Dri. DE72 17 F6
Meath Av. DE21 15 H4
Medina Clo. DE21 21 H3
Medway Dri. DE22 9 G1
Meerbrook Clo. DE21 11 E4
Megaloughton La. DE21 16 A4
Melandre Ct. DE22 13 G3

Melbourne Clo, Allestree. DE22 8 D4
Melbourne Clo, Mickleover. DE3 12 C4
Melbourne St. DE1 6 C6
Melbreak Clo. DE3 12 C6
Melfort Clo. DE24 19 H6
Mellor St. DE24 20 D3
Melrose Clo. DE24 19 H6
Melton Av. DE23 19 F2
Memorial Rd. DE22 8 C3
Mendip Clo. DE21 10 C4
Menin Rd. DE22 8 C3
Mercaston Rd. DE21 10 D5
Merchant Av. DE21 16 B3
Merchant St. DE22 13 G2
Mercian Mews. DE21 16 B3
Merion Gro. DE23 12 D6
Merlin Grn. DE24 19 G4
Merlin Way. DE3 18 A1
Merridale Rd. DE3 19 F1
Merrill Way. DE24 20 D4
Merrybower Clo. DE24 19 F5
*Merthyr Ct, Leominster Dri. DE21 11 F3
Metcalfe Clo. DE24 21 G1
Meynell Ct. DE22 8 C3
Meynell St. DE23 14 A6
Michelle Clo. DE23 19 F5
Michigan Clo. DE21 16 A2
Micklecroft Gdns. DE23 18 C2
Mickleover By-Pass. DE3 12 C6
Mickleross Clo. DE3 12 B4
Middleton Av. DE23 13 F5
Middleton Dri. DE23 13 F5
Middleton St. DE23 14 B6
Midland Pl. DE1 14 D4
Midland Rd. DE1 14 D4
Midway. DE22 9 E4
Milburn Gdns. DE21 11 E3
Milbury Clo. DE21 10 D3
Mileash La. DE22 9 F4
Mileash Ter. DE22 9 F4
Milford St. DE1 6 B1
Mill Clo, Borrowash. DE72 17 F6
Mill Clo, Findern. DE65 18 B6
Mill Croft. DE3 12 B4
Mill Hill. DE24 21 H4
Mill Hill La. DE1 6 B6
Mill Hill Rd. DE23 14 B4
Mill La. DE3 12 B3
Mill Row. DE21 16 C2
Mill St. DE1 13 H2
Millbank Rd. DE21 12 C2
Milldale Rd. DE21 16 D4
Millennium Way. DE24 15 F3
Millers Ct. DE21 6 B1
Millom Pl. DE21 10 B4
Milton Clo. DE3 12 A4
Milton St. DE22 13 G3
Mimosa Cres. DE21 19 G3
Minster Rd. DE21 10 C3
Misterton Clo. DE22 9 E4
Mitcham Walk. DE22 12 D1
Moira St. DE23 11 E6
Molineaux St. DE24 14 C5
Monarch Dri. DE21 11 F3
Moncrieff Cres. DE21 11 E5
Mondello Dri. DE24 21 H3
Monk St. DE22 6 A4
Monks Clo. DE24 19 F5
Monmouth St. DE23 15 E1
Monsal Dri. DE21 16 D4
Montrose Clo. DE24 19 H4
Monyash Clo. DE21 10 D5
Moor Dri. DE24 21 G3
Moor End. DE21 16 D2
Moor La, Ockbrook. DE72 17 F1
Moor La, Osmaston. DE24 20 C3
Moor Rd. DE21 10 C2
Moor Way. DE21 10 C2
Moore St. DE23 14 B4
Moorgate. DE22 12 C2
Moorhead Av. DE24 21 E3
Moorland Rd. DE3 12 B5
Moorside Cres. DE24 20 A4
Moorway Croft. DE23 19 E2
Moorway La. DE23 19 E3
Moray Walk. DE21 10 B6
Morden Clo. DE22 12 D2
Morefern Dri. DE21 10 D4
Morledge. DE1 6 C3
Morleston St. DE23 14 C4
Morley Gdns. DE21 11 E5
Morley Rd. DE21 11 E6
Morley St. DE22 13 F2

Morlich Dri. DE24 19 G4
Morningside Clo. DE24 20 D4
Mornington Cres. DE21 13 E1
Morpeth Gdns. DE21 10 B4
Mortimer St. DE24 20 C1
Mosedale Clo. DE24 21 E1
Moss St. DE22 13 G4
Mossvale Dri. DE23 18 D3
Mostyn Av. DE23 13 F6
Mottistone Clo. DE24 21 H4
Moult Av. DE21 16 C3
Mount Carmel St. DE23 14 B4
Mount St. DE1 6 B6
*Mountbatten Clo, Walton Av. DE24 20 D4
Mountfield Way. DE73 21 H4
Mountford Clo. DE21 11 E3
Mowbray Gdns. DE24 20 C1
Mowbray St. DE24 20 C1
Moy Av. DE24 19 H6
Muirfield Dri. DE3 12 D6
Mulberries Ct. DE22 9 ED2
Mull Ct. DE24 19 G5
Mullion Pl. DE24 21 G3
Mundy Clo. DE1 13 H2
Mundy St. DE1 13 H2
Munro Ct. DE24 19 G4
Murray Rd. DE24 12 C4
Murray St. DE24 21 F1
Muswell Rd. DE22 12 C2
Myers Clo. DE24 20 A5

Nairn Av. DE21 10 B6
Nairn Clo. DE22 13 F4
Namur Clo. DE24 12 B3
Napier Clo. DE3 12 A4
Napier St. DE22 12 A4
Naseby Clo. DE3 12 A4
Nearwood Dri. DE21 10 C3
Neilson St. DE24 21 E2
Nelson Clo. DE3 12 C4
Nelson St. DE1 14 D4
Nesfield Clo. DE24 21 H2
Ness Walk. DE22 9 E3
Netherwood Ct. DE24 8 C3
Nevinson Av. DE23 19 G2
Nevinson Dri. DE23 19 G2
Nevis Clo. DE24 19 G6
New Chester St. DE1 9 G6
New Mount Clo. DE23 19 G3
New Rd. DE22 9 F4
New St, Derby. DE1 14 D3
New St, Ockbrook. DE72 17 F3
New Zealand Sq. DE22 13 F2
Newark Rd. DE21 16 A6
Newbold Av. DE72 17 G6
Newbold Clo. DE73 21 F6
Newborough Rd. DE21 21 H3
Newbridge Cres. DE24 21 E4
Newdigate St. DE23 20 A1
Newel Walk. DE3 12 A6
Newhaven Rd. DE21 16 A2
Newland St. DE1 6 B4
Newlyn Dri. DE23 19 H1
Newmarket Ct. DE24 15 E6
Newmarket Dri. DE24 15 E6
Newport Ct. DE24 21 H3
Newquay Pl. DE24 21 H4
Newstead Av. DE21 15 F2
Newtons Walk. DE22 9 E6
Nicholas Clo. DE23 16 D2
Nicola Gdns. DE23 19 G4
Nidderdale Clo. DE24 21 H2
Nightingale Av. DE24 20 C2
Noble St. DE1 14 D4
Noel St. DE22 13 G2
Norbury Clo. DE22 8 D4
*Norbury Ct, Norbury Clo. DE22 8 D4
Norbury Cres. DE23 19 F3
Norfolk St. DE23 14 C5
Norman Av. DE23 19 G1
Normanton La. DE23 13 F6
Normanton Rd. DE1 6 C5
North Av, Darley Dale. DE22 9 F3
North Av, Mickleover. DE3 12 C4
North Clo. DE3 12 C5
North Par. DE1 6 B1
North Row. DE22 9 F4
North St, Derby. DE1 6 B1
North St, Littleover. DE23 13 F5
North Walk. DE22 9 E6
Northacre Rd. DE21 11 E3
Northfield. DE24 19 F5
Northmead Dri. DE22 13 E4

Northumberland St. DE23 14 B5
Northwood Av. DE21 10 C6
Norwich St. DE21 10 B6
Norwood Clo. DE22 13 E3
*Nothills Clo, Hawksdale DE73 21 F6
Nottingham Rd, Borrowash. DE72 17 F6
Nottingham Rd, Chaddesden. DE21 15 F2
Nottingham Rd, Derby. DE1 6 C2
Nottingham Rd, Spondon. DE21 16 C4
Nuns St. DE1 13 H2
Nunsfield Dri. DE24 21 G2
Nursery Clo. DE72 17 F5
Nutwood Clo. DE22 9 F3

Oadby Rise. DE23 19 G4
Oak Clo, Allestree. DE22 8 D4
Oak Clo, Ockbrook. DE72 17 G
Oak Cres. DE23 19 E
Oak Dri, Alvaston. DE24 21 F
Oak Dri, Mickleover. DE3 12 C
Oak Ridge. DE21 11 E
Oak St. DE23 14 B
Oak Tree Ct. DE72 17 G
Oakdale Gdns. DE21 11 E
Oakham Clo. DE21 10 B
Oaklands Av. DE23 19 F
Oakleigh Av. DE21 15 F
Oakover Dri. DE22 8 D
Oakside Way. DE21 11 E
Oaktree Av. DE24 20 B
Oakwood Clo. DE24 19 C
Oakwood Dri. DE21 11 E
Offerton Av. DE23 19 H
Old Blacksmiths Yd. DE1 6 B
Old Chester Rd. DE1 9 C
Old Church Clo. DE21 8 C
Old Hall Av, Alvaston. DE24 21 C
Old Hall Av, Littleover. DE23 13 E
Old Hall Rd. DE23 13 H
Old La. DE22 9 H
Old Mansfield Rd. DE21 10 A
Old Orchard Wk. DE21 16 B
Old Vicarage Clo. DE23 13
Oldbury Clo. DE21 10
Olive Gro. DE21 15 C
Olive St. DE22 13 H
Oliver St. DE22 13
Olton Rd. DE3 12
Onslow Rd. DE3 12
Opal Clo. DE21 10
Orchard Clo, Boulton Moor. DE24 21
Orchard Clo, Breadsall. DE21 10
Orchard Clo, Littleover. DE23 19
Orchard Clo, Ockbrook. DE72 17
Orchard La. DE21 16
Orchard St, Derby. DE1 6
Orchard St, Mickleover. DE3 12
Orchard Way. DE73 21
Ordish Av. DE21 16
Oregon Way. DE21 11
*Oriel Ct, Bloomfield Clo. DE1 14
Orkney Clo. DE24 19
Ormskirk Rise. DE21 16
Osborne St. DE1 14
Osmaston Pk Rd. DE24 20
Osmaston Rd, Derby. DE1 6
Osmaston Rd, Osmaston. DE24 20
Osnabruck Sq. DE1 6
Osprey Clo. DE24 19
Osterley Grn. DE22 13
Oswestry Clo. DE21 1
Otter St. DE1 6
Otterburn Dri. DE24 2
Oulton Clo. DE24 20
Outram Way. DE24 19
Oval Clo. DE23 19
Overdale Rd. DE23 19
Owlers La. DE23 13
Owlswick Clo. DE24 19

xenhope Clo. DE23 18 C2
xford St, Derby. DE1 14 D4
xford St,
Spondon. DE21 16 C3
xton Way. DE24 19 H6
Oxwich Ct,
Leominster Dri. DE21 11 F3

Paddock Croft, Chandlers
Ford. DE21 10 C4
adley Clo. DE22 9 G1
adstow Clo. DE24 19 F5
adstow Rd. DE24 21 H3
alatine Gro. DE23 18 D1
all Mall. DE23 10 C2
alladium Dri. DE23 18 D2
alm Clo. DE23 13 E6
almerston St. DE23 13 G5
arcel Ter. DE22 13 G3
ares Way. DE72 17 G2
ark Dri. DE23 13 F6
ark Farm Dri. DE22 8 D4
ark Gro. DE22 9 E6
ark Hill Dri. DE23 21 H4
ark La,
Littleover. DE23 13 F6
ark Leys Ct. DE21 16 D4
ark La,
Mickleover. DE3 12 B5
ark Rd,
Spondon. DE21 16 B3
ark St. DE1 14 D4
ark View Clo. DE22 9 E2
arker Clo. DE1 6 A1
arker St. DE1 6 A1
arkfields Dri. DE22 9 E6
arkside Rd. DE21 15 G2
arkstone Ct. DE23 12 A5
arliament Clo. DE22 13 G4
arliament St. DE22 13 G4
artridge Way. DE3 13 E5
astures Av. DE23 18 D1
astures Hill. DE23 13 E6
aterson St. DE21 15 H2
atmore Sq. DE23 19 H2
atten Ct, Wordsworth Dri.
DE24 20 A3
atterdale Rd. DE24 15 G6
avilion Rd. DE23 19 F1
axton Clo. DE3 12 A6
ayne St. DE21 13 G1
each St. DE23 13 G2
acock Clo. DE21 19 E2
ak Dri. DE24 20 B2
ar Tree Cres. DE32 20 B1
ar Tree Rd. DE23 14 B5
ar Tree St. DE23 14 C6
arl Clo. DE21 10 D3
artree Ct. DE21 10 B5
ckham Gdns. DE22 13 E3
ebles Clo. DE24 19 G6
el St. DE22 13 G2
ers Clo. DE21 11 E4
et St. DE22 13 H3
ggs Walk. DE23 19 G2
gwell Clo. DE23 19 G2
lham St. DE22 6 A5
mbroke St. DE21 10 B6
nalton Clo. DE24 21 E3
ncroft Gro. DE23 19 F4
ndennis Clo. DE24 21 G3
ndlebury Dri. DE3 12 C6
ndleside Way. DE23 18 C2
nge Rd. DE22 12 D1
nny Long La. DE22 9 E5
nnycress Clo. DE23 18 D2
nrhyn Av. DE23 13 E6
nrith Pl. DE21 10 B4
ntewen Clo. DE22 9 E3
entland Clo,
Bonnyrigg Dri. DE21 10 D4
nzance Rd. DE24 21 G3
rcy St. DE23 13 H4
regrine Clo. DE24 19 G5
rth Clo. DE3 12 C4
rth St. DE21 10 B4
terborough St. DE21 10 C6
terhouse Ter. DE23 14 C5
terlee Pl. DE24 21 G3
tersham Dri. DE24 21 H2
veril Av. DE72 17 G5
veril St. DE24 20 D2
easant Fld Dri. DE21 17 E1
oenix St. DE1 6 C2
kering Pass. DE21 10 B5
grims Way. DE24 19 F6
ar Ct. DE3 12 C6
nlico. DE22 13 E2

Pinecroft Ct. DE21 11 E4
Pinglehill Way. DE73 21 G6
Pingreaves Dri. DE73 21 F6
Pintail Dri. DE24 19 G5
Pittar St. DE22 6 A6
Plantain Gdns. DE23 19 F4
*Plimsoll Ct,
Warner St. DE22 13 H4
Plimsoll St. DE22 13 F2
Plough Gate. DE22 9 F4
Ploughfield Clo. DE23 19 E2
Pollards Oaks. DE72 17 F6
Ponsonby Ter. DE1 13 H2
Pontefract St. DE24 20 D3
Pontypool Clo. DE21 11 F4
Poole St. DE24 20 D3
Poplar Av. DE21 16 C3
Poplar Clo. DE24 21 G2
Poplar Nook. DE22 9 F2
Poplar Rd. DE72 9 F4
*Porlock Ct, Countisbury
Dri. DE21 10 D4
Porter Rd. DE23 14 B5
Porters La,
Findern. DE65 18 A6
Porters La,
Oakwood. DE21 10 C3
Porters Rd. DE23 13 G5
Portico Rd. DE23 18 D3
Porthcawl Pl. DE21 11 F3
Portland Clo. DE3 12 B5
Portland St. DE23 14 B6
Portman Chase. DE24 19 F6
Portreath Dri. DE22 9 E3
Potter St. DE21 16 C3
Powell St. DE23 13 G5
Poyser Av. DE21 10 D6
Prescot Clo. DE3 12 A6
Prestbury Clo. DE21 11 E4
Pride Pk. DE24 15 E4
Pride Parkway. DE24 14 C3
Priestland Av. DE21 16 B3
Prime Park Way. DE1 6 D1
Primrose Clo. DE21 10 D3
Primula Way. DE24 19 F4
Prince Charles Av.
DE22 12 D2
Princes Dri. DE23 13 E5
Princes St. DE23 14 C6
Princess Dri. DE72 17 E5
Priors Barn Clo. DE72 17 G5
Priorway Av. DE72 17 G5
Priory Gdns. DE21 10 D3
Pritchett Dri. DE21 18 C1
Provident St. DE23 14 B5
Pulborough Gdns.
DE23 18 D2
Pullman Rd. DE23 15 G3
Putney Clo. DE22 12 C2
Pybus St. DE22 13 G1

Quantock Clo. DE22 19 G6
Quarn Dri. DE22 8 C3
Quarn St. DE1 6 A1
Quarn Way. DE1 6 A1
Quarndon Heights. DE22 8 D3
Quarndon View. DE22 8 D3
Queen Mary Ct. DE22 9 F6
Queen St. DE1 6 B2
Queens Dri. DE23 13 F5
Queensbury Chase.
DE23 18 D2
Queensferry Gdns. DE24 20 D4
Queensland Clo. DE3 13 G4
Queensway. DE22 13 F1
Quickhill Rd. DE24 19 F6
Quillings Way. DE72 17 G6
Quintyn Rd. DE24 15 G6
Quorn Rise. DE23 19 G3

Rabown Av. DE23 19 F1
Radbourne La. DE22 12 B2
Radbourne St. DE22 13 F2
Radcliffe Av. DE21 15 F1
Radcliffe Dri. DE22 13 G4
Radford St. DE24 21 C1
Radnor St. DE21 10 C4
Radstock Gdns. DE21 10 C4
Radstone Clo. DE21 11 E3
Raglan Av. DE22 13 F2
Railway Ter. DE1 14 D3
Rainham Gdns. DE21 15 H2
Rainier Dri. DE21 15 G1
Raleigh St. DE22 13 F2
Ramblers Dri. DE21 11 F3
Ramsdean Clo. DE21 10 B5
Ramshaw Way. DE21 15 G4

Randolph Rd. DE23 20 A1
Ranelagh Gdns. DE22 13 E1
Rangemoor Clo. DE3 12 C4
Rannoch Clo,
Allestree. DE22 9 E3
Rannoch Clo,
Spondon. DE21 16 D3
Ranworth Clo. DE24 20 D5
*Rauche St,
Morleston St. DE23 14 C4
Raven St. DE22 13 H4
Ravenscourt Rd. DE22 13 F1
Ravenscroft Dri. DE21 15 G2
Ravensdale Rd. DE22 8 C2
Rawdon St. DE23 14 B5
Rawlinson Av. DE22 20 A2
Raynesway. DE24 15 G5
Raynesway Pk Dri.
DE24 15 H6
Raynesway Vw. DE21 15 G3
Reader St. DE21 16 C2
Rectory La. DE21 10 B2
Reculver Clo. DE21 19 G2
Redcar Gdns. DE21 10 B5
Redland Clo. DE24 20 A4
Redmires Dri. DE73 21 F6
Redruth Clo. DE21 21 H4
Redshaw St. DE1 13 H1
Redstart Clo. DE21 16 D1
Redwing Croft. DE23 19 D1
Redwood Rd. DE24 19 H5
Reeves Rd. DE23 14 C6
Regency Clo. DE23 19 F1
Regent St. DE1 14 C1
Reginald Rd N. DE21 15 G1
Reginald Rd S. DE21 15 F2
Reginald St. DE23 14 C5
Regis Clo. DE21 11 E4
Reigate Dri. DE22 12 D1
Renals St. DE22 6 B6
Renfrew St. DE21 10 C6
Repton Av. DE23 13 G6
Retford Clo. DE21 10 B4
Richardson St. DE22 13 G2
Richmond Av. DE23 19 F1
Richmond Clo. DE21 18 D2
Richmond Rd,
Chaddesden. DE21 15 G2
Richmond Rd,
Littleover. DE23 14 C6
Riddings St. DE22 6 A6
Ridgeway Av. DE23 19 F2
Ridgewood Ct. DE21 10 C4
Rigsby Ct. DE3 12 A4
Rimsdale Clo. DE24 19 G5
Ringwood Clo. DE21 10 D5
Ripon Cres. DE21 10 C5
Rivenhall Clo. DE23 19 E2
Riverside Rd. DE24 15 E3
River St. DE1 6 C1
Robert St. DE1 6 D2
Robin Croft Rd. DE22 9 E2
Robin Rd. DE21 9 F6
Robinia Clo. DE21 11 F3
Robins Cross. DE72 17 F6
Robson Clo. DE24 21 F2
Rochester Clo. DE24 21 F3
Rochley Clo. DE21 10 C3
*Rockbourne Clo, Kendolme
La. DE24 21 H2
Rockhouse Rd. DE24 21 F3
Rockingham Clo. DE22 9 G2
Rodney Walk. DE23 18 C1
Rodsley Cres. DE23 19 F3
Roe Farm La. DE21 15 E1
Roe Walk. DE23 14 B5
Roehampton Dri. DE22 12 D1
Roman Rd. DE1 9 G6
Romsley Clo. DE3 12 A4
Rona Clo. DE24 19 H4
Ronald Clo. DE23 19 F2
Royal Gro. DE21 11 F3
Roosevelt Av. DE21 16 A1
Rosamonds Ride. DE23 19 G1
Rose Av. DE72 9 F4
Rose Hill St. DE23 14 C5
*Roseberry Ct,
Appledore Dri. DE21 11 E4
Rosedale Av. DE24 21 F2
Rosemoor La. DE21 11 E4
Rosengrave St. DE1 6 B5
Rosenheath Clo. DE23 19 H3
*Rosette Clo,
Dahlia Dri. DE21 11 F3
Rosewood Clo. DE21 21 G1

Ross Walk. DE21 10 B4
Rossington Dri. DE23 18 C2
Rosslyn Gdns. DE24 21 F3
Rothbury Pl. DE21 10 C4
Rothesay Clo. DE24 19 G4
Rothwell Rd. DE3 12 B4
Rough Heanor Rd. DE3 12 D5
Roughton Clo. DE3. 18 B1
Roundhouse Rd. DE24 14 D4
Rowan Clo,
Chaddesden. DE21 16 A3
Rowan Clo,
Sinfin. DE24 19 F5
Rowan Park Clo. DE23 19 G2
Rowdith Av. DE22 13 G3
Rowdich Pl. DE22 13 G3
Rowena Clo. DE24 21 E2
Rowland St. DE24 20 D3
Rowley Gdns. DE23 19 F1
Rowley La. DE23 19 F2
Rowsley Av. DE23 13 G6
Roxburgh Av. DE21 10 C6
Royal Clo. DE72 17 F6
Royal Hill Rd. DE21 16 B2
Royal Way. DE24 15 E4
Roydon Clo. DE3 12 A4
Rudyard Av. DE21 16 C2
Rugby St. DE24 15 F6
Ruislip Clo. DE22 9 G1
Rupert Rd. DE21 10 D6
Rushcliffe Gdns. DE21 15 F2
Rushcliffe Av. DE21 15 F2
Rushdale Av. DE23 19 G2
Ruskin Rd. DE1 9 F6
Ruskin Way. DE23 19 E1
Russell St. DE23 14 D6
Russet Clo. DE65 11 E4
*Rutherford Rise,
Morefern Dri. DE21 10 C6
Rutland Clo. DE23 17 G5
Rutland Dri. DE21 12 B4
Rutland St. DE23 14 B6
Ryal Clo. DE72 17 G2
Ryan Clo. DE24 19 G5
Rydal Clo. DE22 9 E2
Rye Clo. DE21 10 C3
Ryedale Gdns. DE23 19 F4
Ryegrass Rd. DE21 11 F3
Rykneld Clo. DE21 18 C2
Rykneld Dri. DE23 18 C2
Rykneld Rd. DE23 18 B3
Rykneld Way. DE23 18 B3
Rymill Dri. DE21 10 C4

Sacheverel St. DE1 6 C5
Sackville St. DE23 20 A1
Saddleworth Wk. DE24 20 D5
Sadler Gate. DE1 6 B3
Saffron Dri. DE21 10 D4
St Agnes Av. DE22 9 E2
St Albans Rd. DE22 13 F4
St Alkmunds Way. DE1 6 B2
St Andrews Vw. DE21 10 C5
St Annes Ct. DE1 13 H1
St Augustine St. DE23 14 A6
St Brides Walk. DE22 13 E1
St Chads Rd. DE23 14 A5
St Clares Clo. DE23 13 G5
St Cuthberts Rd. DE22 13 F4
St Davids Clo. DE22 13 F4
St Edmunds Clo. DE22 13 F4
St Giles Rd. DE23 14 B6
St Helens St. DE1 6 B2
St Hughs Clo. DE22 9 F4
St James Rd. DE23 14 B6
St James's St. DE1 6 C3
St Johns Av. DE21 15 H3
St Johns Dri. DE21 15 H3
St Johns Ter. DE1 6 A2
St Marks Rd. DE21 14 D1
St Marys Bri. DE1 6 C2
St Marys Clo. DE23 21 F3
St Marys Ct. DE1 6 C1
St Marys Gate. DE1 6 B3
St Marys Mews. DE1 6 B1
St Matthews Wk. DE21 9 F4
St Maws Clo. DE3 12 A4
St Mellion Clo. DE21 12 D6
St Michaels Clo. DE65 11 H2
St Michaels Clo. DE24 6 C2
*St Michaels View,
Branksome Av. DE24 21 H2
St Nicholas Clo. DE23 8 D3
St Nicholas Mews. DE1 6 B1
St Nicholas Pl. DE1 6 B1
St Pancras Way. DE1 6 D1
St Pauls Rd. DE1 9 G6

St Peters Church Yd. DE1 6 C4
St Peters St. DE1 6 C4
St Peters Way. DE1 6 C4
St Quenten Clo. DE22 13 F5
St Stephens Clo,
Borrowash. DE72 17 F6
St Stephens Clo,
Sunnyhill. DE23 19 G2
St Swithuns Clo. DE22 13 F4
St Thomas Rd. DE23 14 B6
St Werburghs Churchyard.
DE1 6 B3
St Werburghs Vw. DE21 16 B3
St Wystans Rd. DE22 13 F4
Sale St. DE23 14 C5
Salisbury St. DE23 14 B4
Sallywood Clo. DE24 19 G6
Saltburn Clo. ED21 10 B4
Sancroft Rd. DE21 16 C2
Sandalwood Clo. DE24 21 H2
*Sandbach Clo,
Gleadmoss La. DE21 11 E5
Sanderson Rd. DE21 16 A2
Sandfield Clo. DE21 11 E5
Sandgate Clo. DE24 21 G3
Sandown Av. DE3 12 A4
Sandown Rd. DE24 20 D1
Sandringham Dri. DE21 16 D3
Sandringham Rd. DE21 10 C4
Santolina Dri. DE21 10 D4
Sapperton Clo. DE23 19 F3
Saundersfoot Way.
DE21 11 F3
Saxondale Av. DE3 12 B4
Scarborough Rise.
DE21 10 A5
Scarcliffe Clo. DE24 20 D5
Scarsdale Av,
Allestree. DE22 8 D3
Scarsdale Av,
Littleover. DE23 13 F5
School La. DE73 21 F6
Scott St. DE23 14 B6
Scropton Walk..DE24 21 E5
Seagrave Clo. DE21 11 E5
Seale St. DE1 6 C1
Searl St. DE1 6 A2
Seascale Clo. DE21 10 B4
Seaton Clo. DE3 12 A5
Sedgebrook Clo. DE21 10 C4
Sedgefield Grn. DE3 12 A6
Sefton Rd. DE21 15 F1
Selbourne St. DE24 15 E5
Selkirk St. DE1 10 B6
Selworthy Clo. DE21 10 D4
Selwyn St. DE1 13 F2
Serina Av. DE23 19 G1
Sevenlands Dri. DE24 21 H4
Sevenoaks Av. DE22 12 C2
Severn St. DE24 21 E1
Severn Vale Clo. DE22 9 G1
Seymour Clo. DE23 13 E1
Shacklecross Clo. DE72 17 F6
Shaftesbury Cres. DE23 14 C6
Shaftesbury St. DE23 14 D5
Shaftesbury St Sth.
DE23 14 C6
Shakespeare St. DE24 20 A4
Shaldon Dri. DE23 13 G6
Shalfleet Dri. DE24 21 H3
Shamrock St. DE23 13 G5
*Shandwick Ct,
Cairngorm Dri. DE24 19 G5
Shannon Clo. DE23 19 G2
Shannon Sq. DE21 15 H3
Shardlow Rd. DE24 21 G2
Shaw Grn. DE22 13 G2
Shaw St. DE22 13 G2
Shearwater Clo. DE23 19 G2
Sheffield Pl. DE1 14 D3
Sheldon Ct. DE24 21 E5
Shelley Dri. DE23 20 A3
Shelmorcy Clo. DE24 20 D3
Shelton Dri. DE23 21 E5
Shelton Ter. DE23 13 G3
Shenington Way. DE21 11 E4
Shepherd St. DE23 13 F6
Sheridan St. DE24 20 A4
Sherston Clo. DE21 11 E3
Sherwin St. DE22 8 D6
Sherwood Av,
Borrowash. DE72 17 G5
Sherwood Av,
Chaddesden. DE21 15 G1
Sherwood Av,
Littleover. DE23 13 F4
Sherwood St. DE23 13 H4
Shetland Clo. DE21 10 B6
Shipley Walk. DE24

33

Shire Oaks Clo. DE23 19 F2
*Shirland Ct,
Smisby Way. DE24 21 E5
Shirley Rd. DE21 10 C5
Shorewell Gdns. DE24 21 H3
Short Av. DE22 9 F1
Shottle Walk. DE24 20 D5
*Shrewsbury Clo,
Leominster Dri. DE21 11 F3
Shropshire Av. DE21 15 F1
Siddalls Rd. DE1 6 D4
Siddals La. DE22 9 F2
Siddons St. DE24 21 F2
Sidmouth Clo. DE24 21 H2
Sidney St. DE1 14 C4
Silver Hill Rd. DE23 14 B5
Silver Hill Rd. DE21 16 D4
Silverburn Dri. DE21 10 D4
Silverton Av. DE24 19 F6
Silvey Gro. DE21 16 C4
Simcoe Leys. DE73 21 F6
Simpson St. DE24 21 E2
Sims Av. DE1 13 G2
Sinclair Clo. DE24 19 G5
Sinfin Av. DE24 20 D4
Sinfin Fields Cres. DE24 20 D4
Sinfin La. DE24 20 A4
Sir Frank Whittle Rd.
DE21 9 H6
Siskin Clo. DE3 18 A2
Siskin Dri. DE24 19 G5
Sitwell Clo. DE21 16 C3
Sitwell St,
Derby. DE1 6 C5
Sitwell St,
Spondon. DE21 16 C3
Skiddaw Dri. DE3 12 C6
Skipton Grn. DE21 10 A5
Skylark Way. DE24 19 G4
Slack La. DE22 13 F2
Slaidburn Clo. DE3 12 C6
Slaney Clo. DE24 21 E2
Slater Av. DE1 13 G2
Sledmere Clo. DE24 21 H2
*Slindon Croft, Derrington
Leys. DE24 21 H2
Sloane Rd. DE22 12 D2
Smalley Dri. DE21 11 E3
Smisby Way. DE24 21 E5
Snelford Clo. DE3 12 A4
Snelsmoor La. DE73 21 G6
Snelston Cres. DE23 13 F5
Society Pl. DE23 14 B5
*Solway Clo, Caldermill
Dri. DE21 10 D4
Somerby Way. DE21 10 D4
Somersal Clo. DE24 20 D5
Somerset St. DE21 10 B6
Somme Rd. DE22 8 C3
South Av,
Chellaston. DE73 21 E5
South Av,
Darley Abbey. DE22 9 F3
South Av,
Littleover. DE23 13 F6
South Av,
Spondon. DE21 16 C3
South Brae Clo. DE23 19 F2
South Ct. DE3 12 B6
South Dri,
Chellaston. DE21 15 G2
South Dri,
Chellaston. DE73 21 F5
South Dri, Derby. DE1 9 F6
South Dri,
Mickleover. DE3 12 D5
South St. DE1 13 H2
Southcroft. DE23 19 G4
Southdown Clo. DE24 19 F6
Southgate Clo. DE3 12 A4
Southmead Way. DE22 13 E4
Southwark Clo. DE22 13 E2
Southwood St. D24 21 E1
Sovereign Way. DE21 11 G3
Sowter Rd. DE1 6 C2
Sowter Sq. DE1 6 B3
Spa Ct. DE1 6 B6
Spa La. DE1 6 B6
Sparrow Clo. DE24 19 G4
Speedwell Clo. DE21 11 F3
Spenbeck Dri. DE22 9 G1
Spencer Av. DE24 20 D4
Spencer St. DE24 21 F1
Spindletree Dri. DE21 10 C4
Spinney Clo. DE22 9 F4
Spinney Rd,
Chaddesden. DE21 10 D6
Spinney Rd,
Derby. DE22 13 H5

Spoonleywood Ct. DE23 18 D2
Spring Gdns. DE21 10 D6
Spring St. DE22 6 A5
Springdale Ct. DE3 12 C6
Springfield. DE23 13 E5
Springfield Rd,
Chaddesden. DE21 16 A2
Springfield Rd,
Chellaston. DE73 21 E6
Springwood Dri. DE21 11 E4
Squires Way. DE23 18 D2
Stables St. DE22 13 G2
Stadium Way. DE24 15 E4
Stafford St. DE1 6 A3
Staines Clo. DE3 12 A5
Staithes Walk. DE21 10 A4
Staker La. DE3 18 B2
Staker Way. DE3 18 B2
Stamford St. DE24 20 D3
Stangate Grn. DE3 12 C5
Stanhope Rd. DE3 12 C4
Stanhope St. DE23 14 B5
Stanier Way. DE21 15 G4
Stanley Clo. DE22 9 F5
Stanley Rd,
Alvaston. DE24 21 E2
Stanley Rd,
Chaddesden. DE21 15 G3
Stanley St. DE72 13 G2
Stanstead Rd. DE21 12 A4
Stanton St. DE23 14 A5
Starcross Ct. DE3 12 A4
Statham St. DE22 9 E6
Station Rd,
Borrowash. DE72 17 E6
Station Rd,
Breadsall DE21 10 B2
Station Rd,
Mickleover. DE3 12 B5
Station Rd,
Spondon. DE21 16 B4
Staunton Av. DE23 19 G3
Staveley Clo. DE24 21 E5
Staverton Dri. DE3 12 B4
Steeple Clo. DE21 10 C4
Stenson Av. DE23 19 G2
Stenson Rd. DE23 19 G2
Stephensons Way.
DE21 15 G4
Stepping Clo. DE21 13 G2
Stepping La. DE1 13 G2
Stevenage Clo. DE24 21 F4
Stevenson Pl. DE23 19 E1
Stewart Clo. DE21 16 D2
Stiles Rd. DE24 21 G1
Stirling Clo. DE21 10 B5
Stockbrook Rd. DE22 13 G4
Stockbrook St. DE22 6 A5
Stocker Av. DE24 21 H2
Stone Clo. DE21 16 C2
Stone Dri. DE21 16 A3
Stonebroom Wk. DE24 21 E5
Stonechat Clo. DE3 13 E5
Stonehill Rd. DE23 14 A5
Stonesby Clo. DE21 10 D4
Stonesdale Ct. DE24 21 H2
Stoney Cross. DE21 16 C4
Stoney Flats Cres. DE21 11 E6
Stoney Gate Rd. DE21 16 C4
Stoney La. DE21 16 D3
Stoneyhurst Ct. DE24 21 E5
Stoodley Pike Gdns.
DE22 8 C4
Stores Rd. DE1 10 A6
Stornoway Clo. DE24 19 G5
Stourport Clo. DE73 21 F5
Stowmarket Dri. DE21 10 B5
Strand. DE1 6 B3
Stratford Rd. DE21 10 B4
Strathaven Ct. DE24 16 C3
Strathmore Av. DE24 21 F3
Streatham Rd. DE22 13 E2
Stretton Clo. DE3 12 B6
Stroma Clo. DE24 19 H4
Strutt St. DE23 14 C5
Stuart St. DE1 6 C2
Sudbury Clo. DE1 13 H3
Sudbury St. DE1 13 H3
Suffolk Av. DE21 15 F1
*Summers Ct,
Lodge La. DE21 16 C3
Summerbrook Ct. DE22 6 A5
Summerwood Ct. DE23 19 G2
Sun St. DE22 6 A5
Sunart Clo. DE24 19 H6
Sundew Clo. DE21 16 D3
Sundown Av. DE23 19 G2
Sunflower Clo. DE24 15 G6
Sunningdale Av. DE21 16 C2

Sunny Grove. DE21 15 G2
Sunnydale Av. DE23 19 G2
Sunnyhill Av. DE23 19 G2
Surbiton Clo. DE22 13 E2
Surrey St. DE22 13 G2
Sussex Circus. DE21 10 B6
Sutherland Rd. DE23 14 B6
Sutton Av. DE73 21 E5
Sutton Clo. DE22 13 F1
Sutton Dri. DE24 21 E4
Sutton Ho. DE24 21 H4
Swaledale Ct. DE24 21 H2
*Swallow Clo,
Partridge Way. DE3 13 E5
Swallowdale Rd. DE24 19 G4
Swanmore Rd. DE23 19 E1
Swanwick Gdns. DE21 10 D4
Swarkestone Dri. DE23 19 F3
Swayfield Clo. DE3 12 A5
Sweet Briar Clo. DE24 21 F4
Swift Clo. DE3 13 E4
Swinburne St. DE1 6 B6
Swinderby Dri. DE21 11 E4
Sycamore Av,
Allestree. DE22 8 D2
Sycamore Av,
Findern. DE65 18 B6
Sycamore Ct. DE21 16 C3
Sydenham Rd. DE22 12 D1
Sydney Clo. DE3 12 C4

Taddington Clo. DE21 10 C5
Taddington Rd. DE21 10 C5
Talbot St. DE1 6 A4
*Talgarth Clo,
Leominster Dri. DE21 11 F3
Tamar Av. DE22 8 D2
Tansley Rise. DE21 10 D4
Taplow Clo. DE3 12 A5
Tasman Clo. DE3 12 C4
Taunton Clo. DE24 21 H1
Taverners Cres. DE23 19 F1
Tavistock Clo. DE24 19 F5
Tawny Way. DE23 18 D2
Tay Clo. DE24 19 G6
Tay Walk. DE22 9 E3
Taylor St. DE24 15 E5
Tayside Clo. DE24 19 F5
Tedworth Av. DE24 19 F6
Telford Clo. DE3 12 C6
Templar Clo. DE24 19 F6
Temple St. DE23 14 B5
Templebell Clo. DE23 18 D3
Tenant St. DE1 6 C3
Tenby Dri. DE21 11 F3
Tennessee Rd. DE21 15 G1
Tennyson St. DE24 20 D1
Terry Pl. DE24 21 E2
*Teviot Pl, Bonnyrigg
Dri. DE21 10 D4
Tewkesbury Cres. DE21 10 B5
Thackeray St. DE24 20 A3
Thames Clo. DE22 12 C2
Thanet Dri. DE21 21 F3
Thatch Clo. DE22 9 F3
The Avenue,
Chaddesden. DE21 15 G2
The Avenue,
Derby. DE1 6 C5
The Chase. DE24 20 A4
The Circle. DE24 19 H4
The Close,
Arlington Rd. DE23 13 G5
The Close,
Ferrers Way. DE23 9 F3
The Cock Pitt. DE1 6 D4
The Court. DE24 21 G2
The Covert. DE21 16 C3
The Crescent,
Alvaston. DE24 21 E3
The Crescent,
Chaddesden. DE21 15 F2
The Crest. DE22 9 E4
The Croft. DE23 19 G1
The Eyrie. DE23 19 G5
The Green,
Findern. DE65 18 B6
The Green,
Allestree. DE22 8 D4
The Green,
Mickleover. DE3 12 B6
The Grove. DE3 12 B5
The Hayes. DE65 18 A6
The Hill. DE22 9 F4
The Hollow. DE21 19 F1
The Hollows. DE3 12 B6
The Orchards. DE22 8 D3
The Paddock. DE73 21 H4
The Paddocks. DE72 17 F3

The Parade. DE3 12 B6
The Parker Centre. DE1 9 H5
The Pingle,
Allestree. DE22 9 E2
The Pingle,
Spondon. DE21 16 D3
The Poplars. DE22 9 F2
The Riddings. DE22 9 E2
The Ridings. DE72 17 G2
The Rise. DE22 9 E4
The Settlement. DE72 17 F3
The Sidings. DE21 15 G4
The Spinney. DE72 17 G6
The Spot. DE1 6 C4
The Square. DE3 12 B6
The Underpass. DE1 6 D2
The Walk. DE23 19 G3
Theatre Walk. DE1 6 D4
Thirlmere Av. DE22 9 E2
Thirsk Pl. DE24 20 D2
Thistledown Clo. DE22 9 F3
*Thoresby Clo,
Edwinstowe Rd. DE21 11 E4
Thorn Clo. DE22 8 D2
Thorn St. DE23 14 B5
Thorndike Av. DE24 21 F1
Thorness Clo. DE24 21 H4
Thornhill Rd,
Kingsway. DE22 13 F3
Thornhill Rd,
Littleover. DE23 13 F6
Thorntree La. DE1 6 C4
Thorpe Dri. DE3 12 B4
Thorpelands Dri. DE22 8 D5
Thrushton Clo. DE65 18 A6
Thruxton Clo. DE24 21 H3
Thurcroft Clo. DE22 13 F2
Thurlow Ct. DE21 10 D5
Thurrows Way. DE73 21 G6
Thyme Clo. DE23 19 F4
Tiber Dri. DE24 21 H3
Tickham Av. DE24 19 F6
Ticknall Walk. DE23 19 G3
Tideswell Rd. DE21 10 C5
Tilbury Pl. DE24 21 F3
Tiller Clo. DE23 19 E2
Timbersbrook Clo. DE21 11 E4
Timsbury Ct. DE21 10 C4
Tintagel Clo. DE23 14 C5
Tiree Clo. DE24 19 H4
*Tissington Dri,
Smalley Dri. DE21 11 E3
Tiverton Clo. DE3 12 B4
Tivoli Gdns. DE1 13 H1
Tobermory Way. DE24 19 G5
Tonbridge Dri. DE21 21 F3
Top Manor Clo. DE72 17 G3
Topley Gdns. DE21 10 D4
Torridon Clo. DE24 19 H4
Tower St. DE24 20 D2
Towle Clo. DE72 17 F6
Traffic St. DE1 6 D5
Trafford Way. DE23 19 F1
Tredegar Dri. DE21 11 E3
Trefoil Clo. DE23 18 D1
Tregaron Clo. DE21 11 F3
Tregony Way. DE24 19 G5
Trent Clo. DE24 19 G6
Trent Dri. DE23 19 G3
Trent Rise. DE21 16 D3
Trent St. DE24 21 F1
Trenton Clo. DE21 16 A2
Trenton Grn. DE21 15 H1
Tresillian Clo. DE22 9 E3
Treveris CloL. DE21 16 D3
Trevone Ct. DE24 21 H3
Trinity St. DE1 6 D5
Troon Clo. DE3 18 D1
Troutbeck Gro. DE23 18 D2
Trowbridge Clo. DE21 10 C4
Trowels La. DE22 13 F3
Truro Cres. DE21 10 C5
Trusley Gdns. DE23 19 F3
Tudor Rd. DE21 15 G1
Tufnell Gdns. DE22 13 E1
Tulla Clo. DE24 19 G6
Tuphall Clo. DE73 21 G6
Turner St. DE24 20 D3
Tuxford Clo. DE21 11 E4
Tweedsmuir Clo. DE24 19 G5
Twickenham Dri. DE22 13 E2
Twin Oaks Clo. DE23 18 C2
Twyford St. DE23 6 C6
Tynedale Chase. DE24 19 F6

Uffa Magna. DE3 12 B6
Ullswater Dri. DE21 10 B4

Ullswater Dri. DE21 16
Underhill Av. DE23 20
Underhill Clo. DE23 19
Upchurch Clo. DE3 12
Uplands Av. DE23 19
Uplands Gdns. DE23 13
Upper Bainbridge St.
DE23 14
Upper Boundary Rd.
DE22 13
Upper Dale Rd. DE23 14
Upper Hollow. DE23 13
Upper Moor Rd. DE24 20
Urie Pl. DE24 19
Uttoxeter New Rd. DE22 13
Uttoxeter Old Rd. DE1 13
Uttoxeter Rd. DE3 12

Vale Mills. DE22 6
Vale St. DE23 14
Valley Rd,
Chaddesden. DE21 15
Valley Rd,
Littleover. DE23 13
Vancouver Av. DE21 16
Varley St. DE24 20
Vauxhall Av. DE22 13
Verbena Dri. DE23 19
Vermont Dri. DE21 16
Vernon Dri. DE21 16
Vernon Gate. DE1 13
Vernon St. DE1 13
Vestry Rd. DE21 16
Vetchfield Clo. DE24 19
Vicarage Av. DE23 14
Vicarage Ct. DE3 12
Vicarage Dri. DE21 15
Vicarage Rd,
Chellaston. DE73 2
Vicarage Rd,
Mickleover. DE3 12
Vicarwood Av. DE22
Victor Av. DE22 9
Victoria Av. DE72 1
Victoria Clo. DE3 12
Victoria St. DE1 6
Victory Rd. DE24 20
Village St. DE23 1
Vincent Av. DE21 16
Vincent St. DE23 14
Vine Clo. DE23 19
Viola Clo. DE21 1
Violet St. DE23 1
Vivian St. DE1 9
Vulcan St. DE23 1

Wade Av. DE23 1
Wade Dri. DE23 12
Wade St. DE23 1
Wadebridge Gro. DE24 2
Wagtail Clo. DE24 19
Wakami Cres. DE73 2
Walbrook Rd. DE23 14
Waldene Dri. DE24 2
Waldorf Av. DE24 2
Waldorf Clo. DE24 21
Walker La. DE1 6
Wallace St. DE22 1
Wallfields Clo. DE6 18
Walnut Av. DE24 2
Walnut St. DE24 2
Walpole St. DE21 1
Walsham Ct. DE21 1
Walter St. DE1 1
Waltham Av. DE24 2
Walthamstow Dri.
DE22 1
Walton Av. DE24 2
Walton Dri. DE23 19
Walton Rd. DE21 1
Wansfell Clo. DE3 1
Ward St. DE22 1
Wardlow Av. DE21 1
Wardwick. DE1 6
Warner St, Derby. DE22 1
Warner St,
Mickleover. DE3 1
Warren St. DE24 1
Warwick Av. DE23 1
Warwick St. DE24 1
Washington Av. DE21 1
Waterford Dri. DE21 1
Watergo La. DE3 1
Waterloo Ct. DE1 1
Watermeadow Rd.
DE22 1
Waterside Clo. DE22 1
Watson Gdns. DE1 1
Watson St. DE1 1

Watten Clo. DE24 19 H6
Waveney Clo. DE22 9 G1
Waverley St. DE24 20 C2
Wayfaring Rd. DE21 10 D4
Wayzgoose Dri. DE21 14 D2
Weavers Clo. DE72 17 G6
Weavers Grn. DE3 12 A6
Webster St. DE1 6 B5
Weirfield Rd. DE22 9 F4
Welbeck Gro. DE22 8 D3
Well St. DE1 6 B1
Welland Clo. DE3 12 B4
Wellesley Av. DE23 19 G2
Wellington Cres,
Wellington St. DE1 14 D4
Wellington St. DE1 14 D4
Wells Ct. DE23 18 C1
Wells Rd. DE23 12 C5
Welney Clo. DE3 12 B6
Welshpool Rd. DE1 10 B4
Welwyn Av. DE24 21 E4
Welwyn Av. DE22 8 D3
Wembley Gdns. DE22 12 D2
Wendover Clo. DE3 12 A6
Wenlock Clo. DE3 12 C6
Wensley Dri. DE21 21 H2
Wensleydale Wk. DE24 21 H2
Wentworth Clo. DE3 12 D6
Werburgh Clo. DE21 16 C3
Werburgh St. DE22 6 A5
Wesley Rd. DE24 21 G3
Wesley St. DE72 17 F2
Wessington Mews. DE22 9 E5
West Av,
Chellaston. DE73 21 E5
West Av, Derby. DE1 6 A1
West Bank Av. DE22 9 E5
West Bank Clo. DE22 9 E5
West Clo. DE72 9 E4
West Dri. DE3 12 A5
West Gro. DE24 20 D3
West Lawn. DE65 18 B6
West Park Rd. DE22 9 E5
West Rd. DE21 16 B2
West Row. DE22 9 F4
West Service Rd. DE24 15 G5
West View Av. DE23 19 E1
Westbank Rd. DE22 9 E1
Westbourne Park. DE22 12 C1
Westbury Cl. DE22 13 G4
Westbury St. DE22 13 G4
Westcroft Av. DE23 19 G4
Westdene Av. DE24 20 D3
Western Rd,
Derby. DE23 14 B4
Western Rd,
Mickleover. DE3 12 B5
Westgreen Av. DE24 20 D4
Westhall Rd. DE3 12 B4
Westleigh Av. DE22 13 F2
Westminster St. DE24 21 F1
Westmorland Clo. DE21 14 D2
Weston Park Av. DE24 20 D5
Weston Park Rd. DE24 20 D5
Westwood Dri. DE24 20 D3
Wetherby Rd. DE24 20 D1
Wey Acres. DE72 17 F6
Wharfedale Clo. DE24 9 G2
Wheatcroft Way. DE21 9 H4
Wheathill Gro. DE23 18 D2
Wheatland Clo. DE22 19 F1
Wheatsheaf Clo,
Ryegrass Rd. DE21 11 F3
Wheeldon Av. DE22 9 E6
Wheelwright Way.
DE24 14 D4
Whenby Clo. DE3 12 A5
Whernside Av. DE24 21 H2
Whinbush Av. DE24 21 E4
Whiston St. DE23 14 B5
Whitaker Gdns. DE23 13 G5
Whitaker Rd. DE23 13 G5
Whitaker St. DE23 14 C5
Whitby Av. DE21 10 A4
White St. DE22 9 E6
White Way. DE22 9 E4
Whitecross Gdns. DE1 13 H1
Whitecross St. DE1 13 H1
Whitehouse Clo. DE24 20 D5
Whitehurst St. DE24 20 D3
Whitmore Rd. DE21 15 F1
Whitstable Clo. DE23 19 G2
Whittington St. DE24 20 D3
Whittlebury Dri. DE22 18 D2
Whitwell Gdns. DE24 21 H3
Whyteleafe Gro. DE21 11 E4
Wickersley Clo. DE22 9 E4
Wildybank Clo. DE3 8 C4
Willodale Clo. DE3 12 A5

Wild St. DE1 13 G2
Wildsmith St. DE24 21 F1
Wilfred St. DE23 14 C5
Wilkins Dri. DE24 20 D2
Willesden Av. DE22 12 D1
Willetts Rd. DE21 11 E6
William St. DE1 6 A1
Willn St. DE23 14 B6
Willow Clo. DE72 9 F4
Willow Croft. DE24 9 F4
Willow Row. DE1 6 A2
Willowcroft Rd. DE21 16 C4
Willowherb Clo. DE24 19 H6
Willows End Clo. DE65 18 B6
Willson Av. DE23 19 F1
Wilmington Av. DE23 19 F1
Wilmington Av. DE24 21 G4
Wilmore Rd. DE24 20 A3
Wilmot Av. DE21 15 F2
Wilmot St. DE1 6 C5
Wilmslow Dri. DE21 11 E5
Wilson Clo. DE3 18 A1
Wilson Rd. DE21 10 C5
Wilson St. DE1 6 B4
Wilsthorpe Rd. DE21 15 G1
Wilton Clo. DE24 19 F6
Wiltshire Rd. DE21 10 B6
Wimbledon Rd. DE22 12 D1
Wimbourne Clo. DE73 21 H6
Wimpole Gdns. DE22 13 E1
Wincanton Clo. DE24 9 G3
Winchcombe Way. DE21 11 E3
Winchester Cres. DE21 10 B5
Windermere Cres. DE22 9 E3
Windermere Dri. DE21 16 C2
Windley Cres. DE22 9 F5
Windmill Clo,
Boulton Moor. DE24 21 H4
Windmill Clo,
Ockbrook. DE72 17 G2
Windmill Hill La. DE22 13 F2
Windrush Clo. DE22 9 G1
Windsor Av. DE22 13 E1
Windsor Clo. DE72 17 G6
Windsor Ct. DE3 12 B4
Windsor Dri. DE21 16 D2
Wingerworth Pk Rd.
DE21 16 C3
Wingfield Dri. DE21 10 D4
Winslow Grn. DE21 16 A1
Winster Rd. DE21 10 C5
Wintergreen Dri. DE23 18 D2
Wisgreaves Rd. DE24 21 E1
Witham Dri. DE23 19 G3
Witney Clo. DE24 20 C1
*Witton Ct,
Glenmore Dri. DE24 19 G4
Woburn Pl. DE22 13 E3
Wolfa St. DE22 6 A4
Wollaton Rd. DE24 10 C5
Wolverley Grange.
DE24 21 H2
Wood Rd,
Chaddesden. DE21 10 D4
Wood Rd,
Spondon. DE21 17 E2
Woodale Clo. DE23 18 D2
Woodbeck Ct. DE21 11 E3
*Woodchester Dri,
Keldolme La. DE24 21 H2
Woodcote Way. DE23 18 D2
Woodcroft. DE23 19 G1
Woodford Rd. DE22 12 D1
Woodhall Dri. DE23 18 C1
Woodhurst Clo. DE21 10 B5
Woodland Av. DE72 17 G5
Woodland Rd. DE22 9 E6
Woodlands Av. DE24 21 E4
Woodlands Rd. DE22 9 E1
Woodminton Dri. DE73 21 H5
Woodrising Clo. DE23 11 E3
Woodroffe Walk. DE23 19 G2
Woods La. DE22 6 A6
Woodside Dri. DE22 9 G2
Woodsorrel Dri. DE21 11 E3
Woodstock Clo. DE22 8 D2
Woodthorne Av. DE24 21 E4
Woodthorpe Av. DE21 15 G1
*Woodwards Clo,
Ballards Way. DE72 17 G6
Woolrych St. DE1 14 B5
Worcester Cres. DE21 10 B5
Wordsworth Av. DE24 19 H4
Wordsworth Dri. DE24 20 A3
Wragley Way. DE24 19 F6
Wren Park Clo. DE65 18 B6
Wren Way. DE3 18 A2
Wretham Clo. DE3 18 B1

Wroxham Clo. DE24 20 D5
Wyaston Clo. DE22 9 E4
Wye St. DE24 21 F1
Wyndham St. DE24 21 F2
Wynton Av. DE24 21 E1
Wyvern Way. DE21 15 F3

Yarrow Clo. DE24 19 H6
Yarwell Clo. DE21 10 B5
Yates Dri. DE23 14 B6
Yates St. DE23 14 B6
Yeovil Clo. DE24 19 F6
Yew Tree Av. DE72 17 G3
Yew Tree Clo. DE24 21 H2
Yewdale Gro. DE21 11 F3
York Rd. DE21 15 F1
York St. DE1 13 H2
Youlgreave Clo. DE21 10 C5
Young St. DE23 14 B6
Ypres Rd. DE22 8 C4

Zetland Cres. DE24 19 F6

CASTLE DONNINGTON

Ambassador Rd. DE74 24 C1
Apiary Gate. DE74 24 C2
Argosy Rd. DE74 25 E6
Ashby Rd. DE74 25 E6
Aston Av. DE74 24 B3
Back La. DE74 24 B1
Bakewell Dri. DE74 24 C3
Barroon. DE74 24 C2
Bentley Rd. DE74 24 A1
Beverley Rd. DE74 25 E5
Bondgate. DE74 24 C2
Borough St. DE74 24 C2
Bosworth Rd. DE74 24 A2
Campion Hill. DE74 24 B1
Carrs Clo. DE74 24 C2
Castle Hill. DE74 24 C2
Cavendish Clo. DE74 24 C3
Cedar Rd. DE74 24 C4
Charnock Hill. DE74 24 C6
Charnwood Av. DE74 24 D2
Cheriborough Rd. DE74 24 B3
Church La, Castle
Donington. DE74 24 C1
Church La,
Lockington. DE74 25 E1
Church St. DE74 25 G1
Clapgun St. DE74 24 C2
Cooks Clo. DE74 24 B3
Cordwell Clo. DE74 24 B2
Crabtree Clo. DE74 24 B3
Daleacre Av. DE74 25 F1
Darsway. DE74 24 B1
Delven La. DE74 24 C2
Diseworth Rd. DE74 24 B4
Dove Cote. DE74 24 C2
Eastway. DE74 24 C2
Eaton Rd. DE74 24 C3
Ferrers Clo. DE74 24 B2
Fosbrook Dri. DE74 24 A2
Fox Rd. DE74 24 A1
Garden Cres. DE74 24 C2
Gasny Av. DE74 24 C1
Grange Dri. DE74 24 B2
Grays Clo. DE74 24 A2
Grimes Gate. DE74 24 D6
Hall Farm Clo. DE74 24 C3
Hall Gdns. DE74 25 E1
Hallam Fields. DE74 24 C3
Harcourt Pl. DE74 24 C2
Harvey Ct. DE74 24 C2
Harvey Rd. DE74 24 C2
Hastings St. DE74 24 C3
Haulton Dri. DE74 24 C1
Hawthorn Rd. DE74 24 C1
Hazelrigg Av. DE74 24 B1
*Hemington Ct,
Main St. DE74 25 E1
Hemington Hill. DE74 24 D2
Hemington La. DE74 25 F1
High St. DE74 24 B4
Hill Top. DE74 24 B4
Hillside. DE74 24 C2
Huntingdon Av. DE74 24 C3
Hyams La. DE74 25 F6
Kings Gate. DE74 24 B3
Kirkland Clo. DE74 24 B2
Little Hill. DE74 24 B4
Lockington Rd. DE74 25 E1
Lothian Pl. DE74 24 B2
Loudoun Pl. DE74 24 B2

Main St,
Hemington. DE74 25 E1
Main St,
Lockington. DE74 25 F2
Market Pl. DE1 24 C2
Market St. DE74 24 C2
Meadow Cres. DE74 24 C3
Minton Rd. DE74 24 A2
Moira Dale. DE74 24 D2
Montford Mews. DE74 24 D2
Montieth Pl. DE74 24 C2
Mount Pleasant. DE74 24 C3
Orchard Av. DE74 24 B2
Orly Av. DE74 24 C3
Paddock Clo. DE74 24 A2
Park Av. DE74 24 B2
Park La. DE74 24 A2
Peartree Clo. DE74 24 B2
Queensway. DE74 24 B2
Rawdon Clo. DE74 24 B1
Roby Lea. DE74 24 A2
Routh Av. DE74 24 C3
St Annes La. DE74 24 C2
St Edwards Rd. DE74 24 C3
Salina Clo. DE74 24 B2
Salters Clo. DE74 24 B2
School La. DE74 24 B2
Shields Cres. DE74 24 B3
Shirley Clo. DE74 24 B1
Short La. DE74 24 A1
Spital Hill. DE74 24 B1
Starkie Av. DE74 24 A2
Station Rd. DE74 24 C1
Staunton Clo. DE74 24 B2
Stone Hill. DE74 24 C3
Studbrook Clo. DE74 24 A2
Swan River. DE74 24 C5
Sycamore Rd. DE74 24 C1
Tanyard Clo. DE74 24 C1
The Biggin. DE74 24 C1
The Birches. DE74 24 D6
The Green. DE74 24 C2
The Hollow. DE74 24 C2
The Horse Shoes. DE74 25 E1
The Moat. DE74 24 C2
The Spinney. DE74 24 B1
The Spital. DE74 24 B1
Tipnall Rd. DE74 24 B2
Towles Pastures. DE74 24 B3
Trent La. DE74 24 C1
Victoria St. DE74 24 C1
Viscount Rd. DE74 24 D6
Walton Hill. DE74 24 B1
William Rd. DE74 24 C1
Windmill Clo. DE74 24 C3

CHELLASTON

Aston Clo. DE73 27 C2
Aston La. DE73 27 C1
Back La. DE73 27 C1
Barley Croft. DE73 27 C1
Bensley Clo. DE73 27 C2
Boyd Gro. DE73 27 C2
*Bradmoor Gro,
Netherside Dri. DE73 27 C1
Bridle Clo. DE73 27 C2
Chapel La. DE73 27 C2
Chellaston Pk Ct. DE73 27 B1
Church Clo. DE73 27 C1
Crowland Dri. DE73 27 C1
Davids Clo. DE73 27 B2
Derby Rd. DE73 27 B1
Derby Southern Bypass.
DE73 27 A3
Fellowlands Way. DE73 27 C1
Filbert Walk. DE73 27 C2
Foxdell Way. DE73 27 C1
Glenwood Rd. DE73 27 C2
Green Av. DE73 27 C1
Groves Nook. DE73 27 C1
Hawksdale Clo. DE73 27 C1
High St. DE73 27 C1
Hillnook Clo. DE73 27 C1
Hollymoor Dri. DE73 27 C1
Lady Mantle Clo. DE73 27 C2
Lee Farm Clo. DE73 27 C1
Lincoln Grn. DE73 27 C2
Lockington Clo. DE73 27 B1
Manor Rd. DE73 27 C1
Maple Dri. DE73 27 C1
Meadow Way. DE73 27 C2
Middlebeck Clo. DE73 27 C2
Mill Moor Clo. DE73 27 B1
Moyne Gdns. DE73 27 C2
Netherside Dri. DE73 27 C1
Newgate Clo. DE73 27 D1

*Nothills Clo,
Hawksdale Clo. DE73 27 C1
Orchard Way. DE73 27 B1
Parklands Dri. DE73 27 C2
Parkway. DE73 27 B1
Penhaligans Clo. DE73 27 B1
Penhaligans Wk. DE73 27 B1
Pit Close La. DE73 27 C1
Priory Clo. DE73 27 C2
Ridgeway. DE73 27 C2
Rye Butts. DE73 27 B1
St Peters Rd. DE73 27 C1
Sandyhill Clo. DE73 27 C1
School La. DE73 27 C1
Second Av. DE73 27 C1
Sinfin Moor La. DE73 27 A1
Sladelands Dri. DE73 27 C1
Smallmeer Clo. DE73 27 C1
Snelsmoor La. DE73 27 C1
Stadmoor Clo. DE73 27 C1
Station Clo. DE73 27 B2
Station Rd. DE73 27 B2
Swarkestone Rd. DE73 27 B3
Tarina Clo. DE73 27 C1
Thurstone Furlong.
DE73 27 B1
Townsend Gro. DE73 27 C1
Tudorfield Clo. DE73 27 C2
Walnut Clo. DE73 27 C2
Warrendale Ct. DE73 27 C1
Weston Rise. DE73 27 C2
Willowbrook Grange.
DE73 27 C1
Wimbourne Clo. DE73 27 C1
Woodbridge Clo. DE73 27 B1
Woodgate Dri. DE73 27 C2
Woodlands La. DE73 27 C2
Woodlands Yd. DE72 27 C2
Yews Clo. DE73 27 C1

DRAYCOTT

Albert Rd. DE72 27 C5
Arthur St. DE72 27 A5
Attewell Clo. DE72 27 D5
Belvoir Clo. DE72 27 D5
Breaston Ind Est. DE72 27 D5
Bridge Field. DE72 27 D5
Burlington Clo. DE72 27 D4
Churchill Clo. DE72 27 D4
Cleveland Av. DE72 27 B5
Delamere Clo. DE72 27 D4
Derby Rd. DE72 27 A4
Derwent St. DE72 27 B6
Draycott Rd. DE72 27 B5
Earlswood Clo. DE72 27 D4
Elvaston St. DE72 27 C5
Far Croft. DE72 27 D3
Festival Av. DE72 27 D5
Fowler St. DE72 27 C5
Garfield Av. DE72 27 B5
Gertrude Rd. DE72 27 B5
Gregory Av. DE72 27 C5
Harrington St. DE72 27 C5
Hayes Av. DE72 27 C5
Hills Rd. DE72 27 C5
Hind Av. DE72 27 D5
Holly Clo. DE72 27 B6
Holmes Rd. DE72 27 D4
Hopwell Rd. DE72 27 B4

INDUSTRIAL & RETAIL:
Breaston Ind Est.
DE72 27 D5
Lime Gro. DE72 27 A5
Lodge St. DE72 27 B6
McNeil Gro. DE72 27 B6
Mapleton Rd. DE72 27 B5
Market St. DE72 27 C5
Meadow Clo. DE72 27 B5
Mills Clo. DE72 27 B5
Milner Av. DE72 27 B6
Plackett Clo. DE72 27 D4
Queens Ct. DE72 27 B5
St Marys Av. DE72 27 C5
Sawley Rd. DE72 27 C5
South St. DE72 27 C5
Spring Clo. DE72 27 D5
Station Rd. DE72 27 C5
Stevenson Av. DE72 27 C5
Sydney Rd. DE72 27 B5
The Crescent. DE72 27 C5
The Croft. DE72 27 B6
The Green. DE72 27 C5
Thoresby Cres. DE72 27 A5
Town End Rd. DE72 27 C5
Victoria Av. DE72 27 B5
Victoria Rd. DE72 27 B5

DUFFIELD

Street	Postcode	Ref
Villa St.	DE72	27 C5
Walk Clo.	DE72	27 B6
Wallis Clo.	DE72	27 B5
Walter St.	DE72	27 A5
West Av.	DE72	27 A5
Wilne Rd.	DE72	27 B6
Avenue Rd.	DE56	26 B2
Breedon Av.	DE56	26 B4
Broadway.	DE56	26 B4
Broom Clo.	DE56	26 B4
*Canterbury Clo, New Zealand La.	DE56	26 B4
Castle Hill.	DE56	26 C2
Castle Orchard.	DE56	26 C2
Cavendish Clo.	DE56	26 B4
Chadfield Rd.	DE56	26 C1
Champion Hill.	DE56	26 C3
Chapel St.	DE56	26 C3
Chestnut Clo.	DE56	26 C5
Chevin Bank.	DE56	26 B1
Chevin Rd.	DE56	26 B2
Chevin Vale.	DE56	26 C1
Church Walk.	DE56	26 D5
Crown St.	DE56	26 C3
Cumberhills Rd.	DE56	26 A5
Curzon Ct.	DE56	26 C3
Curzon La.	DE56	26 B4
*Deferrers Ct, Tamworth St.	DE56	26 C3
Derby Rd.	DE56	26 C1
Devonshire Dri.	DE56	26 B4
Donald Hawley Way.	DE56	26 D4
Duck Island.	DE56	26 C3
Eaton Ct.	DE56	26 C5
Ecclesbourne Av.	DE56	26 C4
Ecclesbourne Clo.	DE56	26 C4
Eyes Ct.	DE56	26 C4
Fairlawns.	DE56	26 A4
Ferrers Cres.	DE56	26 A4
Fisher La.	DE56	26 C3
Gilbert Cres.	DE56	26 C5
Golf La.	DE56	26 C1
Granville Clo.	DE56	26 C4
Hall Farm Rd.	DE56	26 C4
Hazel Gro.	DE56	26 B1
Hazeldene Clo.	DE56	26 A1
Hazelwood Rd.	DE56	26 B4
Hill Vw.	DE56	26 B3
Holloway Rd.	DE56	26 C2
King St.	DE56	26 C2
Lime Av.	DE56	26 C4
Lodge Clo.	DE56	26 C4
Makeney Rd.	DE56	26 D5
Marsden Clo.	DE65	26 B4
Mayfair Ct.	DE56	26 C2
Meadow Vale.	DE56	26 A3
Meadows Croft.	DE56	26 B4
Melbourne Clo.	DE56	26 C3
Milford Rd.	DE56	26 C3
Nether Clo.	DE56	26 B1
New Zealand La.	DE56	26 C4
Oak Clo.	DE56	26 B4
Old Hall Av.	DE56	26 B3
Old Mill Clo.	DE56	26 B4
Park Rd.	DE56	26 B4
Philips Croft.	DE56	26 C2
Richmond Av.	DE56	26 B1
St Alkmunds Clo.	DE56	26 C2
St Alkmunds Way.	DE56	26 C2
St Ronans Av.	DE56	26 C4
Scarsdale Rd.	DE56	26 B4
Snake La.	DE56	26 B3
Springfield Dri.	DE56	26 B4
Station App.	DE56	26 C3
Station Rd.	DE56	26 C3
Stiles Walk.	DE56	26 B3
*Tamworth Rise, Tamworth St.	DE56	26 C3
Tamworth St.	DE56	26 C3
Tamworth Ter.	DE56	26 C3
The Pastures.	DE56	26 C3
Town St.	DE56	26 C3
Vicarage La.	DE56	26 C2
Village Ct.	DE56	26 C3
Wiltra Gro.	DE56	26 D4
Wirksworth Rd.	DE56	26 A3

HEANOR LOSCOE

Street	Postcode	Ref
Abbott St.	DE75	23 E4
Adale Rd.	DE75	22 C5
Adams Clo.	DE75	22 D6
Admiral Clo.	DE75	23 E4
Aldercar By-Pass.	NG16	23 F1
Aldercar La.	NG16	23 H1
Aldreds La.	DE75	23 E3
Allandale Rd.	DE75	23 E4
Amber Ct.	DE75	23 H3
Andrews Dri.	NG16	23 G2
Ardsley Clo.	DE75	23 G3
Argyle St.	NG16	23 H2
Ashforth Av.	DE75	23 G5
Ashmount Rd.	NG16	23 H3
Astcote Clo.	DE75	23 G4
Avis Av.	DE75	23 F6
Bailey Brook Cres.	NG16	23 G2
Bailey Brook Dri.	NG16	23 G2
Bailey Brook Ind Est.	NG16	23 H3
Bailey Brook Wk.	NG16	23 G2
Balmoral Clo.	DE75	22 D4
Baker Av.	DE75	23 F6
Banks Burn Clo.	DE75	22 D4
Bassford Av.	DE75	23 F3
Belfield St.	DE75	22 C1
Berle Av.	DE75	23 E3
Bestwick Av.	DE75	23 H4
Birchfield Park.	DE75	23 F6
Birchwood.	DE75	22 D2
Bircum Shaw Rd.	DE75	23 E4
Brampton Av.	DE75	23 G3
Breach Rd, Common.	DE75	22 A2
Breach Rd, Heanor.	DE75	23 G5
Broadway.	DE75	23 E4
Brockhall Rise.	DE75	23 G4
Brook St.	DE75	22 C1
Brooklands Av.	DE75	23 F3
Burns St.	DE75	23 E3
Burnt House Rd.	DE75	23 E3
Burton St.	DE75	23 F6
Buxton Av.	DE75	23 F6
Buxton Grn.	DE75	22 D3
Calladine Clo.	DE75	23 G3
Carlton Clo.	DE75	23 E3
Carlyle Pl.	DE75	23 E3
Carlyle St.	DE75	23 E3
Castle Vw.	NG16	23 G1
Chapel St.	DE75	23 G5
Chestnut Bank.	NG16	22 D4
Chestnut Rd.	DE75	23 G2
Church St.	DE75	23 F4
Church Vw.	DE75	22 C2
Claramount Rd.	DE75	23 G4
Clarke Av.	DE75	22 D3
Claxton St.	DE75	23 E4
Claxton Ter.	DE75	23 E4
Clay La.	DE75	23 F3
Clayton Gro.	DE75	22 D1
Codnor-Denby La.	DE75	22 A1
Coppice Dri.	DE75	23 F6
Corfield Av.	DE75	23 F6
Cottage Gdns.	DE75	22 D3
Cromford Clo.	NG16	23 G1
Cromford Rd.	NG16	23 G1
Daltons Clo.	NG16	23 G1
*Darfield Dri, Brampton Av.	DE75	23 G3
Deepdale Ct.	DE75	23 E5
Delves Rd.	DE75	22 D5
Denby Common.	DE75	22 A3
Derby Rd.	DE75	22 D4
Dodford Ct.	DE75	23 G4
Douglas Av.	DE75	22 D3
Draycott Clo.	DE75	22 C1
Dumbles La.	DE75	22 A3
East Nelson St.	DE75	23 E3
Eastview Ter.	NG16	23 H2
Ebenezer St.	NG16	23 H2
Edward St.	NG16	23 H2
Egreaves Av.	DE75	22 C1
Ella Bank Rd.	DE75	23 G4
Elmsfield Av.	DE75	23 G3
England Cres.	DE75	23 G3
Fairview.	DE75	23 E4
Fall Rd.	DE75	23 E3
Fast St.	DE75	23 G5
Flamstead Av.	DE75	22 C2
Fletcher St.	DE75	23 E3
Ford Av.	DE75	22 C1
Frederic Av.	DE75	23 F6
Frost Av.	DE75	23 G2
Furnace La.	DE75	23 F3
Garnett Av.	DE75	23 H2
George St.	NG16	23 G5
Gillot St.	DE75	23 F3
Gladstone Av.	DE75	23 F3
Gladstone St.	DE75	22 C3
Glue La.	DE75	23 E4
Godfrey St.	DE75	23 G1
Godkin Dri.	NG16	23 G1
Grace Cres.	DE75	23 E4
Grammer St.	DE75	22 B1
Grandfield St.	DE75	22 D1
Greenacre Av.	DE75	23 G3
Greenfields.	NG16	23 G1
Greggs Av.	DE75	23 F3
Gregory Dri.	NG16	23 G2
Groome Av.	DE75	22 C2
Hallington Dri.	DE75	22 D4
Hampden St.	NG16	23 H2
Hands Rd.	DE75	23 F4
Hardy Barn.	DE75	23 G6
Harold Av.	NG16	23 H2
Hassock Lane N.	DE75	23 H6
Hazel Clo.	DE75	22 D4
Heanor Gate Rd.	DE75	22 D5
Heanor Rd, Denby Common.	DE75	22 A2
Heanor Rd, Heanor Gate.	DE75	22 B6
Heanor Rd, Loscoe.	DE75	22 D2
Heyford St.	DE75	23 E3
High St, Heanor.	DE75	23 E3
High St, Loscoe.	DE75	22 C1
Highgrove Clo.	DE75	22 C4
Hill Rd.	DE75	23 E4
Hillside.	NG16	23 G3
Hogbarn La.	DE75	23 G3
Holbrook St.	DE75	23 G2
Holmes Clo.	NG16	22 D3
Holmesfield Dri.	DE75	23 F5
Homestead.	NG16	23 H1
Horsley Cres.	NG16	23 G2
Howitt St.	DE75	23 F4
Huftons Ct.	DE75	23 G6
Huftons Dri.	DE75	23 G6
Hunt Av.	DE75	23 F3
Ilkeston Rd.	DE75	23 F4
INDUSTRIAL & RETAIL:		
Bailey Brook Ind Est.	NG16	23 H3
Sawmills Ind Pk.	DE75	23 E2
Joan Av.	DE75	23 E3
John St.	DE75	23 E3
Johns Pl.	DE75	23 F3
Johnson Dri.	DE75	23 H4
Julie Av.	DE75	22 D4
Kensington Av.	DE75	22 D4
Kew Cres.	DE75	23 H5
Kings Clo.	DE75	22 D4
Kingsway.	DE75	22 D4
Kirkham Clo.	DE75	23 E5
Kirkman Rd.	DE75	22 C1
Lacy Fields Rd.	DE75	23 G4
Lake Av.	DE75	22 D1
Lawn Clo.	DE75	23 F3
Leafy La.	DE75	23 G4
Lee La.	DE75	23 H4
Leniscar Av.	DE75	23 E5
Lockton Av.	DE75	22 C2
Loscoe Grange.	DE75	22 D2
Loscoe Rd.	DE75	23 E3
Loscoe-Denby La.	DE75	22 B2
Lower Claramount Rd.	DE75	23 G4
Lower Dunstead Rd.	NG16	23 H3
Lower Gladstone St.	DE75	23 E3
Lowlands Lea.	DE75	23 F3
Mansfield Rd.	DE75	23 F4
Maple Gdns.	DE75	22 D4
Marina Rd.	DE75	22 C5
Market Pl.	DE75	23 F4
Market St.	DE75	23 E4
Marshall St.	DE75	23 G3
Mayfield Av.	DE75	23 E4
Midland Rd.	DE75	23 E3
Mill Rd.	DE75	23 G5
Millbank. DE7.	DE75	23 G5
Milward Rd.	DE75	22 D3
Mitchell Av.	NG16	23 G2
Mount St.	DE75	23 E4
Mundy St.	DE75	23 E4
Mundys Dri.	DE75	23 F5
Nelson St.	DE75	23 E3
Newham Clo.	DE75	23 G4
Newlands Dri.	DE75	23 F3
Nook End Rd.	DE75	23 E4
North St.	NG16	23 H2
Northern Rd.	DE75	23 D3
Oak Av.	NG16	23 H1
Oakalands Av.	DE75	23 G3
Old Coppice Side.	DE75	23 E6
Oliver Clo.	DE75	23 H3
Orchard Rise.	DE75	23 F3
Orchard St.	NG16	23 H3
Ormonde St.	NG16	23 H1
Ormonde Ter.	NG16	23 H1
Owers Av.	DE75	23 F6
Park St.	DE75	22 D3
Park Vw.	DE75	22 D4
Peach St.	DE75	23 E5
Peatburn Av.	DE75	22 C3
Peel St.	NG16	23 H3
Piatts Av.	DE75	22 D4
Pine Av.	NG16	23 G2
Plumptre Rd.	NG16	23 H1
Poynter Clo.	DE75	22 D4
Princess Clo.	DE75	22 D3
Prospect Rd.	DE75	23 G5
Purchase Av.	DE75	22 D3
Queens Av.	DE75	22 D3
Ray St.	DE75	23 E4
Red Lion Sq.	DE75	23 E4
Regent St.	NG16	23 G6
Ridgeway.	DE75	23 F5
Roper Av.	DE75	23 F4
Rosewood Cres.	DE75	23 H3
St Laurence Clo.	DE75	23 F4
Sawmills Ind Pk.	DE75	23 E2
Saxton Av.	DE75	23 F3
Sedgewick St.	NG16	23 H3
Sheldon Rd.	DE75	22 C1
Sinclair Clo.	DE75	22 D5
Slack La.	DE75	23 E5
Smeeton St.	DE75	23 H4
Smith Dri.	NG16	23 G2
Sovereign Way.	DE75	22 D4
Spring La.	DE75	23 E4
Stainsby Av.	DE75	23 E5
Stamford St.	DE57	23 E3
Starthe Bank.	DE75	23 G4
Station Rd.	NG16	23 H3
Stoddard Dri.	DE75	23 F4
Sunningdale Av.	DE75	23 F6
Tantum Av.	DE75	22 D1
Taylor La.	DE75	22 D?
The Beeches.	DE75	22 C5
The Hamlet.	DE75	23 E3
The Meadows.	DE75	23 E4
The Nook.	DE75	22 C?
Thistle Green Clo.	DE75	23 H4
Thompson St.	NG16	23 H2
Thorpe Rd.	DE75	23 E?
Thorpehill Dri.	DE75	23 F6
Tudor Falls.	DE75	23 E3
Turner Av.	NG16	23 G2
Turton Clo.	NG16	23 G2
Twyford Clo.	DE75	23 G4
Upper Barn Clo.	DE75	23 F?
Upper Dunstead Rd.	NG16	23 H?
Upper Nelson St.	DE75	23 E4
Upton Clo.	DE75	23 G4
Victoria Av.	DE75	22 D
Watkinson St.	DE75	22 D
Watson Av.	DE75	23 F?
Welldon St.	DE75	22 B?
Wellington St.	DE75	22 D
Wentworth Croft.	DE75	23 G
West St, Heanor.	DE75	22 D?
West St, Langley Mill.	NG16	23 H?
Western Dri.	DE75	23 F
Westfield Av.	DE75	23 F
Weston St.	DE75	23 G
Whysall St.	DE75	23 E
Wilmot St.	DE75	23 E
Wilson Av.	DE75	22 C
Windsor Clo.	DE75	23 E
Woodend Rd.	DE75	23 E

LITTLE EATON

Street	Postcode	Ref
Alfreton Rd.	DE21	7
Barley Clo.	DE21	7
Bermuda Av.	DE21	7
Brooks Hollow.	DE21	7
Buxton Dri.	DE21	7
Campwood Clo.	DE21	7
Chatsworth Dri.	DE21	7
Church La.	DE21	7
Coxbench Rd.	DE21	7
Crabtree Hill.	DE21	7
Croft End.	DE21	7
Derby Rd.	DE21	7
Duffield Bank.	DE21	7
Duffield Rd.	DE21	7
Eaton Bank.	DE21	7
Haddon Dri.	DE21	7
Highfields Rd.	DE21	7
Holm Av.	DE21	7
Horsley La.	DE21	7
Little Eaton By-Pass.	DE21	7
Moor La.	DE21	7
Morley La.	DE21	7
New Inn La.	DE21	7
New St.	DE21	7
Old Barn Clo.	DE21	7
Park Clo.	DE21	7
Park View.	DE21	7
Port Way.	DE21	7
Rigga La.	DE21	7
Station Rd.	DE21	7
The Chase.	DE21	7
The Hawthorns.	DE21	7
The Hollies.	DE21	7
The Leys.	DE21	7
The Oaks.	DE21	7
The Town.	DE21	7
Toad La.	DE21	7
Vicarage La.	DE21	7
Westley Cres.	DE21	7
Whittaker La.	DE21	7
Windy La.	DE21	7
Woodlands Clo.	DE21	7
Woodlea Gro.	DE21	7